Put It All Together

Put It All Together

developing inner security

MAURICE E. WAGNER, Th.M., Ph.D.

ZONDERVAN PUBLISHING HOUSE
OF THE ZONDERVAN CORPORATION
GRAND RAPIDS, MICHIGAN 49506

DEDICATION

This book is dedicated to my dear wife who has been a real companion and loving assistant in uncovering the veiled schematic of life's delicate balances.

Contents

Preface

Feelings of insecurity plague the secret thoughts of many people. Their fulfillment in living is dwarfed by the menacing feeling that something dreadful is about to happen. If it doesn't happen today, it may surely happen tomorrow!

Feelings of insecurity also relate to uncertainties about how one may be handling life situations. "What will *they* think? is a haunting uncertainty. "How do I look?" and "How am I doing?" are questions which seem never to be answered satisfactorily for the insecure person.

There are two sides to the problem of emotional disturbance. One is affectual and the other is ideational. The affectual side relates to feelings of anxiety and hostility and guilt. The ideational side relates to a person's sense of identity and self-concept. This volume is concerned with developing inner security, coping with various emotions and how they affect personal relationships. The other side of the problem will be discussed by the author in a companion volume, *Building an Adequate Self-Concept.**

Many people who are insecure emotionally can read and benefit by the information. This book is written in non-technical language for those persons who are seeking some assistance in resolving their own feelings of insecurity, and for those persons who want to improve their understanding of emotional problems in order to be helpful to others.

The insights presented here have been distilled from eight-

*To be published by Zondervan.

een years as a pastor serving three churches, four and one-half years as a Chaplain in one of America's larger Veterans Neuro-Psychiatric hospitals, twelve years as a professional counselor dealing with emotional problems of people from all walks of life, and from special psychological training.

Overcoming emotional insecurity is actually a growth process. Inadequate ways of coping must be overcome and new ways of tackling life situations must be learned. It is something like climbing a ladder. As one reaches for new steps, he must release the step on which he presently stands. As one gains new insights, he must release old attitudes and habits of thinking. Usually it is much more difficult to let go of the familiar which is inappropriate than it is to take hold of the new and challenging, but seizing the new and releasing the old are of equal importance.

It is the author's sincere hope that the information shared in these pages will prove useful to many who have been trying to "put it all together" but who are not really sure of the divine plan for fulfillment in living. They tend to feel at loose ends trying to cope with the perplexing uncertainties which indwell most circumstances, and they would appreciate a few dependable pointers to direct them through this chaotic collage called life before the inevitable problems of aging rob them of ever having truly lived.

1

Security Is a State of Mind

Harry entered my counseling room perplexed. He sat down and anxiously braced himself against the cushions of the sofa. I remarked, "Something seems to be bothering you today." "Yes," he replied cautiously, "something is bothering me. I've been trying to figure *me* out. Sounds crazy, doesn't it—a person my age talking like this." Harry hesitated thoughtfully, then continued, "That's what's wrong with me—I'm never really sure of myself—just who I am. I guess I'm trying to find *me*. It's ridiculous, but that's the way it is. Regardless of how good I feel at times, there's always something missing. I never get hold of a secure feeling about myself. When I seem to, and that is rare, something always happens to take it away."

Many people are like Harry. Some are more articulate in explaining their feelings than others. Everyone welcomes the comfortable feeling of inner security, of a peace of mind, that particular poise which gives one confidence in facing the unexpected situations of life.

Security vs. anxiety

Security and anxiety play teeter-totter. When security is

up, anxiety is down; when anxiety is up, insecurity prevails.

Think for a moment how much we manifest anxiety in our daily concerns. We scan the newspapers, watch television newscasts, and keep our radios on to catch news of developments at the war fronts of the world. We are interested in riots and strikes which threaten national economy. Instantly our attention is riveted to headlines about floods, fires, hurricanes, earthquakes, and plane disasters. Methodically we lock our doors and windows when we leave home, fasten our seat belts and drive defensively. We buy insurance and then, ironically, worry about what might happen next.

A few people defend themselves against feelings of anxiety by avoiding newscasts. They skip over the headlines of their newspaper to read the sports section, the society news, the ads, or the funnies.

Alfred was one of these people. He explained, "I don't like to hear about all the world's troubles. It upsets me. I'm happy not knowing what's going on. I get all I want to know from hearsay. It may be a make-believe world I live in, but I like it that way."

Need for security is universal

Everyone has his own way of trying to make himself feel more secure. Some people withdraw to themselves. Some tend to attack in anger and try to overpower the situation. Some tend to pity themselves for having so many overwhelming problems. Others depend upon their skills in cunningly manipulating the situation. Sometimes these habitual devices work; sometimes they do not.

The need for inner security is universal. From the time we are born many frightening things happen to disturb inner security. Some situations suggest the possibility of sudden death. Fear and anxiety lie at the heart of all insecure feelings, and there is almost always a feeling of aloneness in life connected with anxiety.

Security must be a timeless feeling. Inner security rests on the elbows of yesterday, finds a place to relax today, and yet looks forward optimistically to fulfilling tomorrow's goals.

No one can feel secure when a time limit is imposed upon his hope.

Security relates to inner wholeness

There is a way to live that increases inner security, and there is a way that perpetuates anxiety and emotional insecurity. Security is actually a state of mind. It is first internal before it is external. If a person will think of his *way* of coping with life as the primary problem and will do his best to discover how to deal with situations more constructively, he will be increasing his inner security. If, on the other hand, he allows himself to become preoccupied with the uncertainties in situations and treats these as the primary problem, he will be perpetuating his insecurities and pampering his anxieties. When a person is not secure within himself, he can never find security in his environment.

We find an illustration of this fact when we visit a retirement complex surrounded by high stone walls and a guard at the gate. Every precaution has been made to protect the residents from danger. Much forethought has been given to their every comfort. Situationally, they are made as secure as possible. Does the situation give them inner security? At first there is a sort of honeymoon period of happiness, but after they have become adjusted to their new surroundings, these people evidence about the same level of anxiety they always have had. Each one brings into the environment the anxieties he had previously. If he feared loss of money or health, he still does. If he was suspicious of others, he still is. If he expected people to reject him, he still does. As long as his mind is capable of functioning normally, the retired senior citizen retains about the same level of emotional insecurity he has always had even though his environment may seem ideal.

How you feel does matter

We often find people who tend to suppress their natural emotions. They practice a rigid self-control, for they believe if they control their emotions they are more secure. Other people may express their feelings freely. These people are often regarded as more insecure, but actually it is often the ones who tend to be stoic who are the more insecure. One person's anxieties are simply more apparent than the other's.

Emotion is an evidence of life. We live with our emotions as well as in a turbulent world of colliding interests and competitive priorities. If we can cope with our internal disturbances, we can handle our external perplexities much better. What is happening in our feelings makes the difference. It is impossible to handle stresses from within if we don't have creative courage springing from a sense of inner wholeness. Actually, the world of our emotions presents a far more devastating array of insecurities than the unpredictable, formidable world of circumstances.

Few consider the significance of security

Other concerns seem more important than emotional security; yet emotional insecurity baffles and cripples many lives, obstructs happiness, and triggers prolonged psychosomatic illnesses. The possibility of becoming mentally ill plagues the imagination of more than a few people. Most of this worrisome concern is needless, but it continues because people do not understand themselves or the meaning of life sufficiently to deal with this kind of anxiety.

As a rule, people are more concerned with their economic security than with any other problem. They have certain ambitions and have involved themselves with indebtedness to the limit of their credit, gambling on continuing in good health and holding their job. As a result of this continual financial pressure, their anxieties dictate that if they could only make more money, they would enjoy more security. Usually it is not until some crisis occurs, perhaps a serious illness, a nervous breakdown, a death, that people stop to consider the significance of their own inner security and how their immaturities perpetuate their anxieties. Financial involvements are often related to a person's emotional insecurity.

Relationships with others play a vital part in inner security. For generations we have been too busy to be personally interested in each other. Many people do not know what it is to have just *one* person with whom they feel unguarded, emotionally intimate. They may have many friends, but no one really close. Some people are engaged in ministering to the needs of others and yet have no one with whom they can share their own inner feelings. Instead of home being a place of rest and recuperation with a delightful climate of people enjoying each other, family tensions harass and interfere with any pleasure they might enjoy together.

Usually, if we don't learn how to manage life before we reach adulthood, we become too busy trying to survive in the "rat race" to give serious study to self-improvement. Children need the security of personal loving relationships with their parents and others in the family circle. If they are not loved, they become immature adults who give birth to other immature adults. We become more and more self-centered in our relationships with others and thus more and more insecure. We continue repeating the same mistakes over and over again.

Few people ever expect to collapse emotionally, but nearly everyone ignorantly perpetuates habits of thinking and patterns of behavior which undercut his own inner security. His self-defeating ways, like driving a car with the brakes on, depletes valuable resources of nervous energy. Life becomes dwarfed in fulfillment, work becomes just an endless duty to be maintained for survival. Life is so daily it's boring.

If people only realized that life means growth! To stop growing emotionally is to cease living creatively and autonomously. We may reach the age of physical maturation, but we never live long enough to stop growing up emotionally and spiritually. Regression begins when we think we've "made it."

When a person gets caught up in his past either with nostalgia or with regrets, and loses the sense of challenge in the present, or his sense of creative purpose in the future, he stops growing emotionally. Life becomes boring and uninteresting. He is only living with a partial self-fulfillment. This condition motivates a person to become overwhelmed with self-concerns. He may try to escape from his boredom, but he needs creative introspection. Some try to escape through indulging in inordinate sensual pleasures or in the acquisition of things or in engaging in activities excessively. There is an excitement in new adventures which can prevent one's own immaturities from seeming important.

"I think I'm doing all right"

Everyone cherishes his own viewpoint. The way he is in the habit of thinking and reacting seems to him to be the best. It is right that a person have a healthy self-confidence and feel right about himself. But once in a while something happens, even to the most confident, to pull the rug from under him, and he has to admit there must be a better way.

Many of us settle for less in life when we could have had so much more!

I am thinking of George. He was relatively successful in business. He opened his own auto repair shop, serviced all makes, kept six mechanics busy. George was an aggressive person who projected strength and reliability. He managed his men like an army sergeant, demanding a high quality of performance. He tried to manage his home the same way, but he did not realize that he hadn't learned to share himself with others. Sharing and caring is what home is all about. George was a good man. He never intended to hurt his wife and children, but he did.

After sixteen years of marriage, Martha, his wife, became unable to function because of anxiety. She was so exceedingly depressed and discouraged with life she had considered destroying herself. Their two teen-age children were rebellious, disrespectful, and getting into more and more trouble with the law.

George sent Martha to me for psychological help, but it was not long before I was able to get George in for an interview. After discussing Martha and her anxieties, he told me how disappointed he was with life. He explained that he had finally managed to get his business developed to a point where he and his family could begin to enjoy living and doing things together. Now they weren't interested, and Martha wasn't able.

Finally George exclaimed, "There's got to be a better way! Where have I gone wrong?"

Fortunately, for George, he did stop to reconsider himself and his self-defeating ways. In counseling he learned many things about himself and how to share himself with his family. He recovered most of his losses before it was too late.

Martha was most encouraging. She responded immediately to George's renewed interest in her total person and in his family. "Finally," she said, "after all these years, I feel like George's wife. I've always felt like a second fiddle. His business was all he ever seemed to care about."

It's not a sign of moral weakness to feel anxious or fearful, depressed or overwhelmed. It may be a sign of real emotional need. The pressures of life can become dreadfully threatening when the inner braces are not strong enough to withstand them.

Everyone normally has some anxiety, and it is nothing unusual to feel over-burdened with life's problems. The emotionally secure have a way of "rocking with the boat" and of sustaining themselves until they can rest in quieter waters. The emotionally insecure seldom feel free from anxiety. They are bothered by most everything and tend to resent the fact that life has problems. They are basically wary of life.

What is emotional insecurity?

Usually the person who is emotionally insecure wonders why some people are less anxious than he. He has never felt really secure, so he tends to think of himself as having an unusually hard time. It would be rare insight for an emotionally insecure person to discover that his insecurity is more related to his own personality development than it is to his unfortunate circumstances.

An emotionally insecure person is plagued with manifold anxieties. He tends to feel life is *only* a struggle for survival. The more secure person awakens with, *"Another day, O Lord!"* The insecure person awakens with, *"O Lord, another day?"*

The insecure person feels helpless and unable to cope

with the competitive struggles of life. He has a tremulous uncertainty about who or what he is. He is uncertain about his abilities, his judgments, his ideals. The insecure person is uncertain of his relationships with people and he is ever trying to find an acceptable attitude or a behavior that is worthy of praise. He never knows whether or not his natural feelings are the best feelings to have.

Often the insecure person ruminates about the past. He asks himself, "Why did I say that?" or exclaims, "I should have said so and so," or "If I only had it to do over. . . ." He seems to be trying to change something that has happened to make it better. His concern for the past serves more to fulfill his need to be self-critical than it does to give him an opportunity to learn how to cope better in a future situation.

The secure person looks at his world as basically a friendly place with only an occasional enemy. The insecure person views the same world and hopes somewhere to find a friend. He lives in constant anticipation of disapproval, but wishes at the same time to be complimented and admired.

Emotional insecurity has extremes of intensity. To some it is a way of life; to others it is a recurring crisis.

Sometimes an insecure person can obtain an unusual amount of help from reading a book such as this one. Most of the time, however, an extremely insecure person needs the personal attention of a skilled professional counselor to help him develop needed insights concerning his personality distortion. This book is not written primarily for the extremely insecure, but for those who are occasionally overcome with unrealistic anxiety and who know that their level of insecurity is handicapping them, keeping them from being fulfilled. If they felt better about themselves, they could be more productive and more delighted with their social and personal relationships.

Sometimes insecurity and its emotional disturbances can cause poor physical health. Anxiety can rob a person of sleep, disturb his eating habits, produce indigestion, heart pain, headaches, and a multitude of psychosomatic illnesses. Strangely, however, a person can actually be emotionally secure when his body is in poor health. Peace of mind is not entirely dependent upon good physical health.

As you read this book, please be patient with yourself. Each insight is important, but a person can only change a little at a time. You may want to find the magic wand that will transform you into the secure person you wish to become, but if you are ever to achieve inner security, you must grow into it, and growth is always slow. All you can do is what you can do. As you work at improving, and as you persevere in that ambition, before long you will begin to recognize a new *you* emerging in various ways of coping with life.

2

Be True to Yourself

The first step in discovering inner security is to acknowledge your own emotions—be true to yourself. This may be the hardest task you've ever undertaken. Most of us deny our emotions which we consider to be less acceptable and substitute other emotions which seem more pleasing. We have been trained in childhood to do this by our parents, who meant us no harm. "You *love* your brother. You don't *hate* him, do you?" "Give him a big hug." "Tell the man you're sorry." "Smile, now. Let's be happy." "Tell the lady thank you." Perhaps none of these expressions of emotions represented how we felt at the time, but we tried to comply with the wishes of our parent.

This is how self-deception begins. By nature children are not deceptive; they usually express just how they feel. Parents become apprehensive about this and train them to do otherwise. Then as a child grows to adulthood, he is trained to suppress certain emotions for the sake of being polite, respectful, and proper. There is usually a way of saying something fitting to the occasion without actually lying to yourself and to the others present, but this, unfortunately, is not often emphasized. Instead, for instance, of declaring how

21

much you enjoyed the evening when actually you were bored, it might be better just to thank your host for the time together, or keep still. Graciousness need not be a reason for telling a lie.

But parents do more than just tell us to express a more acceptable emotion. They often forbid emotion: "Stop being angry. Stop it! you hear." A person who succeeds in stopping his anger feelings is scheduling himself for emotional problems later. Anger should be controlled, not stopped. It is common for parents to humiliate their child for being natural. "Don't cry! Be strong. You're acting like a baby!"

Sometimes children are made to feel embarrassed by their desire for affection. Alice remembered how her father used to humiliate her by saying, "Don't be so mushy. Your kisses are too sloppy." This hurt her deeply.

Occasionally a parent's attitude does lasting damage. Alice recalled running to her father when she was ten as she had always done to greet him upon returning from work. She leaped into his arms and hugged him violently, and he peeled her off of himself and exclaimed, "Don't do that anymore. You're a big girl now." From that time on, she never hugged her father, nor did he hug her. She felt guilty for wanting affection.

Children customarily follow the example of their parents. They use them as models. When the parents do not express emotion freely, the child copies their pattern as though he were being taught that free expression is something dangerous or evil. If the parents are freely demonstrative, the children are likely also to accept their own emotions.

Children learn to deny their normal fears and subdue their honest tears. Society places a sort of moral implication on the expression of tears and fears. This is unfortunate. It tends to make people try to force themselves to be unnatural and unexpressive, or to try to force themselves to have emotions that are unnatural.

In discovering inner security, it is important to reclaim forbidden emotions and to accept them as natural. The emotions you have repressed may not be totally unacceptable.

Some of them may be more disturbing than others, but you need to be in touch with your feelings before you can find a better sense of wholeness and a more stable security.

Think logically. How can you develop inner unity when you are denying a part of yourself as real, or trying to feel something you are not feeling?

Don't deny feeling anxious

Whenever we try to prove we are not anxious when we know very well that we are, we condition our minds so that we cannot overcome the problem that makes us anxious. The only remedy is to discover the self-deception and try to be honest. If these hidden, denied feelings can be admitted as real and good in themselves, then we can develop an appropriate way of expressing them. Sometimes talking about how you feel can get you started feeling, and it can at the same time help you hold the necessary control. For instance, saying, "I want you to know that this is making me very angry," is better than to strike out in angry words. "This is making me feel bad" is better than "I feel bad."

When you are trying to recapture unacceptable feelings, I suggest that you avoid asking yourself the usual question, "Why do I feel that way?" It is not important to know *why*: it is only important that you know *how* you feel. If you stop to ask why, you will stop your feelings from emerging into awareness. Later, much later, when you are used to feeling certain unacceptable feelings, it will be quite obvious *why* you feel that way.

The person who wants to become more secure emotionally must be true to himself. This fact cannot be overemphasized. Anxiety and tension will not go away just because a person refuses to believe they exist.

As an example, I think of Marjorie. She never liked horror movies. They terrified her. Her boy friend invited her to a show. She did not realize it was a horror movie until they drove past the theater marquee. She wanted to call the date off, but she was afraid he would make fun of her or reject her. She instantly decided she was not afraid of horror movies, that they were only moving pictures anyway, not real. Notice, she did not try to overcome the fear; she denied she had it. Naturally, she did not enjoy her evening. Her boyfriend thought she was not happy to be with him and felt rejected. Their relationship became strained.

If Marjorie had simply admitted her fear of such movies, she would have been true to herself. She might have admitted to her friend that she feared he would make fun of her. Her friend would have better understood her reaction. By his reaction to her honest admission of feelings, she could have learned much about the personality of her boy friend and discovered what her next move should be in their relationship. She lost a great deal by denying her feelings.

We cannot avoid being controlled by our feelings at times. If we do achieve the goal of stoicism, we tend to be cold, unrelating, and insensitive to the feelings of others. When we find ourselves governed excessively and unrealistically by our feelings, we may do things impulsively that we later regret. The happy medium between over-control and no control might be considered "emotional maturity."

Feelings are important, but they are emotional reactions to something that is either happening outside in the situation or inside within our own psyche. We become involved empathically in various happenings where people are involved. Sometimes we feel defensive. We also become afraid when it seems we are approaching a situation in which previously we have experienced some sort of pain. It is common, for instance, to fear contracting a sore throat or having a tooth extracted.

Don't deny feeling guilty

We all need self-esteem to function at our best. The Bible says, "Do not be conceited, or think too highly of yourself; but think your way to a sober estimate based on the measure of faith that God has dealt to each of you" (Rom. 12:3, N.E.B). This passage indicates that there is a level of self-esteem that is healthy and profitable and that is attainable.

When our self-esteem is diminished by something we say

or do, or by something another person says or does to us, we automatically become anxious, at times fearful and tense, frequently angry. We have lost a measure of self-esteem. Embarrassment is a threatened loss of self-esteem. Guilt is another emotional by-product, and it happens when we admit that the loss of self-esteem was our own fault. We all try instinctively to maintain a secret image of ourselves that has worth. When we lose our sense of worth, we feel we are nothing. The mind cannot bear to feel a sense of nothingness, or badness, or no worth.

This is why it is so hard to admit our faults, unless, of course, the situation provides some compensatory sense of virtue for doing so. For instance, when at a meal you accidently spill some food on your clothes, you often remark, "Look at what I've done. I'm so careless." The virtue lies in the anticipated understanding and forgiveness of the viewers.

When we admit a fault, we usually sacrifice self-esteem and a sense of worth. Usually our guilt feelings are so related in our thinking to our identity that we not only *do* a bad deed but become a bad person.

Unresolved guilt is a root cause of many feelings of insecurity. When we hold ourselves accountable to ourselves, and we naturally do as adults because we are self-governing and responsible persons, we can scarcely forgive ourselves. We have an abiding memory of how we violated our better judgment and gave in to our illicit desires. If we did it once, or more times, we find it impossible to be absolutely sure we won't do it again.

The way to deal with guilt effectively will be discussed fully in a later chapter. For now we need to observe how we perpetuate our insecurity by denying our faults. When we say a fault is not there, it doesn't mean that we are actually guiltless, but that we refuse to be responsible. We refuse to accuse ourselves. This is not being true to ourselves.

The person who never accepts blame never changes, for he sees no need to change. The person who accepts blame excessively and unrealistically also never changes, for he is never specific about what his fault really is. The problem with guilt is just this: To accept blame is to lose self-esteem and become bad or nothing. Not to accept blame is to perpetuate the evil, because there is no acknowledgment of the mistake, and so no correction.

Devices commonly used to avoid guilt

There are a variety of devices the average person uses to avoid the loss of self-love in admitting blame. With each device the person is untrue to his emotions and is sustaining his insecurity.

1. *Projection.* The person who is "always right" whether he is wrong or not has little anxiety about himself, for he has denied his guilt. His guilt is projected to others. He must make others feel guilty whether they are wrong or not. He tends to blame *them,* considering *them* to be difficult and unreasonable and uncooperative. They seem to him to be the cause of his problem and he resents them for it.

Just because a person projects his guilt to others does not make him a more secure person. He is anxious about how well others will cooperate with him. He tends unrealistically to expect others to do what he wishes without considering their feelings in the matter. He really has no basis for inner security, though he bolsters his self-esteem by priding himself in how well he is doing. He continually relies on others and delegates his work to them, trying to manage them, when actually he has no essential control of them. He attempts to coerce them to do what he schedules for them so he can hold on to his self-esteem by being in command. If he succeeds, he has reason to wonder if they will do it for him again; if he fails, he can become angry, or depressed, or withdrawn.

The person who avoids his guilt feelings by projecting to others is in a vicious cycle. Since he denies his responsibility for his own faults, he must continue to prove to himself that he is not guilty by finding fault with others. This critical attitude destroys his relationship with others and motivates them either to strike back or withdraw from him. He needs their good will, yet he must criticize. People's willing cooperation is his primary resource for self-esteem. As he loses friends and tries to make new ones, he tends to become more and more conceited, arrogant, and accusing if things don't go his way.

2. *Self-condemnation.* The opposite kind of personality is one who extracts a peculiar reward from accepting blame for nearly everything that goes wrong. When some problem arises or something fails, his first thought is, "I must be to blame. What did I do wrong?" This kind of self-accusing person preserves his self-love by exaggerating his sense of responsibility for the happenings of life until he doesn't know just what his real guilt is. By blaming himself for everything, he becomes guilty of nothing. Because he is unspecific about his actual faults, yet quickly assumes the blame when there is no evidence that he is at fault, he really never blames himself for much of anything.

The person who tends to blame himself excessively is actually hostile and is passively expressing his anger by the self-criticism. Usually, when a person is angry he will try to make the other person feel bad and undesirable by attacking his self-esteem. The self-condemning person is blaming himself out of spite, not because he actually feels wrong. Instead of making the other person feel bad and undesirable as an expression of his anger, he gives the other person a bad and undesirable person to be with by defacing himself.

As proof of what I have just said, notice for yourself how the person who keeps blaming himself seems to enjoy the efforts other people extend trying to prove to him that he is not as bad as he says he is. This is anger in reverse. Ordinarily, the one who is accused tries to justify himself; this person refuses to accept justification. He is not feeling guilty as he presumes; he is only frustrating those who try to prove his innocence.

3. *Rationalization.* This is a very common way of avoiding guilt feelings. It is an attempt to change absolute right and wrong to a relative value. The person reasons like this: "How bad is it? Who said it is wrong? How does the law

have anything to do with my situation? Others do much worse. Perhaps it's not very bad."

4. *Displacement.* This is another common device. "He made me do it!" or, "I couldn't help myself." These are a displacement of blame away from self. Adam used this device in the Garden of Eden when he and Eve sinned. "The woman whom thou gavest to be with me, she gave me of the tree, and I did eat" (Gen. 3:12). He not only displaced his responsibility to Eve, but he projected blame to God by implication, "The woman thou gavest to be with me...."

5. *Excuses.* Offering excuses is a shield from guilt. I once heard that an excuse is the skin of a reason stretched over a lie. Sometimes, however, excuses are valid, but often they are a blatant avoidance of guilt. "I didn't mean to." "I didn't know better." "Nobody told me." All of these are typical excuses we offer.

6. *Promises.* Promises may be used to avoid guilt. "I'll never do it again," or "I'll do better next time," seem to quiet the conscience. The promise preserves self-esteem because it contains the fantasy of the whole problem being already resolved. The intoxicated person promises to stop drinking, but seldom puts his promises into effect. Since his attention is on the solution through wishful thinking, he doesn't consider it a present problem he needs specifically to work to overcome. The wishful thinking has relieved his anxiety while preparing him to fail again.

7. *Intellectualization.* Some people intellectualize their guilt away. This is an attempt to preserve self-esteem by talking about the fault from various viewpoints until all the bad feelings are dissipated. The person becomes tired of discussing it. Nothing constructive has been implemented to correct the deficiency.

8. *Parade good deeds.* Most of us have a tendency to call attention to the good we have done or intend to do when dealing with guilt. This helps to increase feelings of self-esteem and to minimize the sting of guilt. Emphasizing the good does not erase the bad. It is right to do good.

9. *"That's the way I am."* This is a statement of total

irresponsibility. In effect the person is saying, "I have a right to be deficient, or even to be wrong. Don't blame me." The one who says this has no intention of correcting the problem.

10. *Self-pity.* When all else fails, we instinctively turn to the device we used when we were infants—self-pity. Self-pity is an illusive way of preserving self-love. When we feel sorry for ourslves, we are actually implying that "it" out there is to blame, not I. "I am an innocent victim of circumstances." I am innocent because I am being unjustly overloaded. "It" is bad because "it" is unreasonable and tyrannically demanding. "It" is unkind and unfair to helpless, innocent "me."

As we have just noticed, people who avoid feeling responsible for what is realistically theirs to manage aren't helping to correct the cause of their anxiety and insecurity. They continue to apply juvenile and infantile ways of coping when faced with adult situations. It is impossible to pour a quart of water into a pint jar. Behavior that is acceptable in childhood will not serve in adulthood—the level of responsibility is much greater.

In developing inner security, it is essential to be true to your emotions. Emotions reflect the effect of experience upon both the conscious and unconscious aspects of our mentality. If we deny a natural emotional reaction and repress it, we are actually refusing to acknowledge a part of ourselves. Once a denial is established, it must be maintained, and this takes energy. This energy is used on an unconscious level, but it produces nothing constructive. When a person stops denying some emotion and it returns from the repressed, that is, when he acknowledges his true feelings, he usually is relieved and exhilarated because energy has been set free to be consumed in some useful service.

The substitution tactic

We not only deny anxiety and guilt, but we often make substitutions for these and other emotions. We make substitutions for anger. It is not always easy to be true to oneself when temper is aroused. Anger is a dangerous emotion, for it can destroy valuable objects, hurt cherished relationships, and incur the wrath of others and their condemnation.

Most of us have been told in childhood to control our tempers, and many of us have been punished for losing our temper. Anger can be suppressed—that is, it can be controlled and expressed in such a way as not to harm anyone. When anger is denied, it is instantly repressed into the unconscious. The person no longer feels angry, but feels some other way.

For instance, Marsha was being reprimanded by her teacher. She felt the teacher was unfair, but she dared not express her feelings of rage, so she denied them. She smiled courteously and thanked her teacher for explaining so clearly where she had been wrong on the test. But as soon as she left the classroom, she was in an ugly mood. The rest of the afternoon she slammed doors, kicked furniture, and was disagreeable. She had repressed the feeling of anger toward her teacher, but she gave the feelings that belong to her anger to the doors and furniture. She did to them what she would have liked to do to her teacher. The inanimate objects were safer targets.

Anger needs to be faced as anger, but sometimes the mind makes a substitution for the sake of safety. It is not uncommon for anger to be expressed as guilt. We mentioned this substitution earlier in this chapter when we discussed excessive guilt, or self-condemnation.

Bertha made this substitution frequently. "Bill stood me up last night," she explained. "He never even phoned to let me know he wasn't coming for me. If I were any good, he would have considered me important enough for at least a phone call."

Carl said, "When I begin to feel angry, I also begin to feel guilty and ashamed. I guess it's because I think it's a weakness to get angry, and I am showing how weak I am when I begin to lose my temper."

Life was a struggle for Alex. He was a faithful worker, but often depressed. When he was young, he pouted. His parents would not allow him to express anger. His wife told me that she never knew her husband to be angry, and they had been married twenty-three years. Alex had learned as a child to substitute depression for feelings of anger. Discouragement also stood in for his anger as well as guilt.

On rare occasions it is possible to observe generosity as a substitute for anger, even as it is used for guilt. Mark was in his forties and very emotionally insecure. He related early in his first interview, "I never hate anyone. I love everybody. To illustrate let me tell you what happened when I was just ten years old. A bully in our neighborhood kicked me in the shins. Oh, it hurt! But I didn't hit him or try to get even like most kids would have done. I didn't hate him; I loved him. I went to the store and bought him a candy bar and gave it to him." Little did Mark realize at that time how he was promoting his insecurity by such self-deceptive thinking.

Other substitutions are made. Anger can be a mask for fear. Fear can be so dominant an emotion that it blots out guilt. Anger also substitutes for guilt. Sadie became very angry in one of her first counseling sessions and began to walk out. I asked her what happened. She replied, "You made me feel guilty, and I always get furiously angry when anyone implies that I am wrong."

Emotionally secure people accept responsibility

Emotionally secure persons can admit when they are wrong, and they immediately try to rectify the damage responsibly. An insecure person will try to avoid his responsibilities.

The easiest way to avoid responsibility for one's anger is to say "You make me angry." No one *makes* us angry; we choose to be angry ourselves. There is always a split second in the situation when we willfully choose anger as our reaction. When you begin to own your true reaction as your chosen reaction, you are on your way to wholeness and emotional security.

As anyone tries to face himself realistically and own up to how he feels in each situation, he opens the way to grow stronger and more mature. Then he can do a better job next time being true to himself. When we catch ourselves

denying an emotion or a responsibility, it becomes harder
to practice the self-deception the next time.

Self-deception works best when we are unconscious of it.
As soon as we realize what we are doing, we begin to set in
motion other ways of coping with that kind of situation. This
is how growth takes place.

3

Know Your Security Emotions

In the process of discovering inner security, it is not only essential to be true to yourself in admitting to your genuine emotional reactions, but it is also important to understand something about the dynamics of these emotions. Emotions are legion in number and classification, but our concern here is only with those particular emotions which relate intrinsically to feelings of security or insecurity.

How the mind works

Have you ever wondered just how your mind works? Nearly everyone has given some thought to the subject. We commonly hear our friends say, and perhaps we have also said things like this: "I wish I could remember names when I'm introduced to someone. That's the way my mind works—I forget what I should remember and remember what I should forget." "I wish my mind worked like Bill's—he has a photographic memory." "I don't know what's the matter with me —my mind just won't function this morning. I must have a few dead cells, or something." "I have a one-track mind. It ought to be four-track or stereo. I can only think of one thing at a time."

Much careful study has been given the mind, and we have learned a great deal about its complexities, but there is much more to know. Let us distill a few basic concepts from the research literature in order to comprehend our own thought processes better. We will need to clarify our thinking about ourselves if we are to rehabilitate our emotional life toward strengthening our feelings of inner security.

Mental processes are generally classified into three groups of activities: feeling, knowing, and wishing.* Since our primary concern is with *feeling* secure, we will devote our first attention to the activity of feeling.

Feelings are spontaneous sensations in the body. Emotions are feelings of an instinctive character, and they have both physical and psychical manifestations. In other words, emotion is not just a body sensation; it combines how I want to feel with some underlying basic need. "I feel happy" is a statement of emotion. The body sensations are pleasant, alert, perhaps feeling strength. The mind is at ease, peaceful. " I feel sad" is a statement of an opposite emotion. The body sensations are apathy, dullness, perhaps weakness; the mind is anxious and grieved. Some need has been frustrated. Each emotion can be dissected into a physical feeling and underlying need.

Feelings relate themselves to ideas. An idea is a mental image or concept. Thoughts are usually a blending of feelings and ideas. Feelings are charged with energy. Ideas, in a crude sense of speaking, package the feelings so they can be verbally communicated. It is possible to have ideas without feeling, but it is not natural to do so. A person who does this is denying his feelings and being only intellectual in what he is saying. Sometimes we hear ideas, but we don't understand what is being said until we can get some feeling about the ideas. Then we experience the idea and we remember it. We say we "understand" when we feel the idea.

It is also possible to have feelings without ideas, but this usually happens when we feel flooded or overwhelmed by

* Leland E. Hinsie and Robert J. Campbell, *Psychiatric Dictionary,* Third Edition, Oxford University Press, Inc., 1960.

emotion. When we weep we are usually expressing feelings without much idea structure. We feel overpowered by our emotions.

Feelings and ideas are normally associated together as we experience daily situations. In the process of thinking called repression, the ideas and the feelings are separated. The ideas are denied and removed from awareness and then kept from awareness. The feelings, being disassociated from their ideas, attach themselves to other objects unrelated to the original ideas.

As an example of how this works, recall the story of Marsha in Chapter 2 (she was being unfairly reprimanded by her teacher). She had an instinctual impulse to defend herself against being wronged. Her emotion was rage or hostility. Her feeling was anger, but expressing her anger feelings required that she contradict another basic need—the teacher's good will. Her mind instantly valued the teacher's good will above the need to defend. The internal conflict was resolved by denying the idea of anger, so it was repressed out of her awareness. She no longer felt angry. To keep the anger out of her awareness, she patronized the teacher by complimenting her. This idea maintained the denial of anger. But her feelings were floating about without an object of identity. This was her ugly mood. Her kicking of furniture and slamming of doors was a way of finding a non-threatening object, something very different from the teacher, upon which to vent her feelings so they would have some meaning. Marsha knew these objects were not to blame for anything, but she had to vent her ugly mood somewhere.

When repression takes place, the person is not conscious that it has happened. When one suppresses an emotion, he is conscious of trying to control his emotion or keep it from showing or controlling him.

Though repression is an unconscious process, it can be voluntarily reversed. If Marsha had stopped to reconsider her unrealistic behavior, she might have asked herself some questions. "Why am I behaving this way? I am not angry with doors and furniture. Why am I angry?" Then she could have recalled the incident with the teacher and returned to her angry feelings. As soon as she felt angry again with her teacher, the repression would be lifted. It would be safe at this later moment to reconsider her motives for being angry and patronizing and decide if she were as unfairly treated as she had felt. In the process of this rumination she would probably arrive at some conclusions that would help her face her teacher more realistically, if the situation should occur again. Instead of allowing herself to feel abused by unfair treatment, she might have developed the ability to hold her negative feelings until she had asked some clarifying questions, giving her teacher the benefit of having no desire to treat her unfairly. If the teacher had realized how Marsha really felt, she probably would have treated her differently.

Whenever we return to the emotion we have denied, we set in motion certain mental processes which make the repression less likely to happen again.

Reality in two worlds

Every normal person has five senses with which he perceives the world about him. Sight, sound, and smell are distance perceptors, touch and taste are contact perceptors. With this basic equipment we have five input channels to our process of *knowing*. Our minds record a visual image and an auditory image in the composition of an idea. If there is an odor, we add an olfactory image. Touching and tasting, as this is possible, adds two more dimensions to the composite mental picture of an object. All of these inputs blend together harmoniously, for each is of separate importance. They merge into one sense of knowing, one concept. This concept is stored by memory in our library of knowledge.

When we read back from memory, we describe our knowledge of an object by referring to input from these channels. "The mountains were beautiful," we say, describing a recent camping trip. "The air was scented with spring. Birds were chirping merrily in the treetops. It all made me hungry for that plateful of bacon and eggs frying on the open fire."

The world about us is perceived in these five ways. This knowledge becomes the structure of thought life and of word symbols to express feelings. For the sake of brevity, we will call the world about us "it." "It" is everything we perceive as separate from ourselves. The world we will call "I" is our internal world of mental activity, composed generally of feeling, knowing, and wishing.

We have explained feeling and knowing. We need to clarify what is meant by wishing. A wish in this sense is more than just a desire or a want that is somewhat embellished by imagination. A wish is an impulse, an urge, a striving, a desire, a purpose, or a tendency. This is a more psychological meaning for the word "wish."

Wishes usually express themselves in the mind by fantasies. A fantasy may be described as a moving concept, a daydream. If a concept were a snapshot, a fantasy would be a moving picture.

Fantasies perform an important mental function. In fantasy we are able to preview an expected happening and make important decisions regarding our involvement. In fantasy we plan and create schemes we put into practice. In fantasy we anticipate danger and prepare to protect ourselves.

Fantasies also help us face tomorrow with the hope that it will be a better day than today. I have a dental appointment tomorrow. I know it is going to hurt, but it will soon be over and my mouth will feel good again.

"It" is the source of supply for our basic needs. We depend upon "it" for survival. We perceive "it," and our impressions become a permanent memory. As we experience "it," "it" becomes a vital part of "I."

"It" contains people who are likewise depending upon "it" the same as we. They are part of our "it," and we are a part of theirs. "It" is not only a resource for gratification, but "it" is also a source of frustration, deprivation, rejection, humiliation, hazard, pain, misery, even death. "It" is larger and more omnipotent than "I," and "I" must regard it respectfully and realistically if needs are to be met, and especially if "I" am to feel secure in "it."

Keep the two worlds in balance

There is a dynamic balance that must be maintained between "I" and "it." "It" demands that "I" assume certain responsibilities and do a little giving if "I" am to receive from "it." I have a right to expect that "it" will gratify when these basic requirements are met. The regulations which are fundamental to the dynamic balance between "I" and "it" are known as civil laws, codes of ethics, morals, customs. If I am at the dinner table and ask you to pass the salt, I have a right to expect that you will stop what you are doing and pass the salt. This would be good table manners.

If this dynamic balance is not maintained, conflict results, and sometimes with lasting consequences. If I disregard certain physical laws, I can be seriously hurt. "It" has an established way of regarding me as an object. Other people also have a way of regarding me as an object. If I become too possessive or dominating, people will rebel and refuse to cooperate with my desires. We must live and let live. This is why the Bible clearly defines the basic rule for living with people to be: "As ye would that men should do to you, do ye also to them likewise" (Luke 6:31). This is how God advises us to maintain this dynamic balance.

Further on in Jesus' famous Sermon on the Mount, other words of advice concerning this balance are given: "Judge not, and ye shall not be judged" (Luke 6:37). "With what judgment ye judge, ye shall be judged: and with that measure ye mete, it shall be measured to you again" (Matt. 7:2). This explains the immediate natural reaction of "it" to negative, critical feelings in "I."

On the other hand, if we do good to others and treat them positively, we will receive a positive, good response. "Give, and it shall be given unto you; good measure, pressed down, and shaken together, and running over, shall men give into your bosom. For with the same measure that ye

mete withal it shall be measured to you again" (Luke 6:38).
My attitude has much to do with how "it" responds to "I."

How emotions develop

From the day of our birth, we learn to cope with what
seem to be uncontrollable and unpredictable elements in "it."

We began life as a tiny, helpless infant under the providential care of loving parents. They had the sovereign power
of giving or withholding, of hurting or helping. We were
totally dependent. Because of our total, absolute helplessness,
and their position of absolute control of the supply of our
needs, our interaction with them developed in us the ability
to relate to them as authority figures. Though obedience was
not at first a primary consideration because of our helplessness, obedience did become an essential experience just as
soon as we were able to exercise a will of our own in oppo-
sition to theirs.

Our parents taught us the fundamentals of relating to "it."
They taught us by example, and they taught us by command, and by restriction and punishment. We learned how
to get things for ourselves and we learned how to wait for
others to get things for us. We learned the difference between good and bad, right and wrong, and the principles
of sharing and caring.

Our first emotional responses probably began with the
feeling of air against our bodies just as we were born, the
sound of our own voice crying, and the feeling of being
handled. Hunger was probably the first significant painful
experience. Hunger and its discomfort kept recurring, and
our parents consistently gratified it with food and soothed
our sufferings. The prompt, gracious attention of our parents
at this very early age conditioned our minds to *expect* "it" to
respond to our wishes. As adults, if we want something, we
expect to get it somehow. If it doesn't happen, we tend to
feel frustrated until we understand why.

A reflection of these early impressions is seen occasionally
in adult conversation. "You know very well what I like. If
you loved me, you would do it for me." When we feel a

need or have a desire that someone might be able to satisfy, we automatically expect him to supply it, especially if that person professes to love us. If he doesn't supply, we can feel rejected and angry.

As we grew a little older, perhaps into our second year, we were able to move about and get things for ourselves. We soon learned that there were some things we could do and some things we could not, some things permissible and some things forbidden. We learned to anticipate correction or punishment if we did not follow the explicit commands of our parents. We were taught to control our processes of elimination and many other things. "Be careful, don't spill your milk." We were taught orderliness, to do things a certain way, at a specific place and time. Most of us were taught that we were good if we were obedient and bad if we weren't. We learned, often to our sorrow, how to control our parents and to maneuver around some of their restrictions. Being obedient gave us the fundamentals of the feeling of responsibility.

The sense of expectancy we learned in the first year became a demand in the second. We had learned to expect our parents to supply our needs at first, but later when we were conscious of feeling in control and responsible, this expectancy grew to become a masterful demand for service. This initiated a period of intense power struggle between us and our parents to determine who would be the master.

The consistent, firm controls of the parents at this stage of development is very important to a child's sense of security. A sense of responsibility to parents for certain tasks, a sense of confident self-control, and a sincere respect for authority figures develop during this power struggle period. The power struggle usually lasts into the late teens. People who are emotionally insecure are often either weak or over-developed in these three areas: responsibility, self-control, and respect for authority. The child who is indulged and habitually gets his way learns very little about responsibility, self-control, and respect for authority. The child who is over-restricted and over-controlled usually fears exercising his initiative, is timid and overly anxious.

When parents correct their child in anger, they interfere with the basic love relationship needed with the parent for the child to develop a healthy sense of responsibility. The anger of the parent arouses anger in the child and makes him want to defy their authority over him, though at the same time he may repress his anger because of the fear of his parent's punishment. He cannot feel responsible to them when basically he feels defiant of them. This conflict sponsors emotional insecurity of varying degrees.

In the period of extreme dependency, the child ideally learns to expect "it" to be interested in his needs and ready to supply them, so he can find satisfaction for his desires. This is a basic trust in the goodness of life and the reliability of "it" to supply. This trust is very essential to inner security, and it is derived from the parents' consistent attention, affection, and acceptance of their child.

In the second period when the child develops responsibility, self-control, and respect for authority, he learns that he can find satisfaction for certain of his desires if he uses his initiative and creative imagination. This develops another awareness which is very essential to inner security, and that is a sense of autonomy. By the time a child is three, he should have begun to establish two awarenesses: "I can depend on my parents," and "I can do things for myself."

The power struggle with parents is not always resolved satisfactorily because of the anger the child represses. This is why parents should not completely stop or forbid their child from expressing his emotion. While the emotion may be unacceptable in certain settings, there should be some place arranged where the child can talk openly with his parents and resolve those feelings.

"Don't you ever say you hate your parents. I never want to hear you say that again!" This kind of statement can force a child to repress the feeling he has and then act hatefully or overly compliant without knowing why. A better response from the parent would be, "You feel you hate me. Why?" Let the child explain his case, and thus answer his problem. Then, perhaps, explain. "Sometimes you feel you hate me because you do not get just what you want, but you also love me too. You can stop hating, because it is right for you to obey me."

We sometimes hear adults who have not outgrown their own childhood power struggle period, demanding of others such things as: "If you loved me, you'd let me do as I please." "Nobody tells *me* what to do!" "I have a right to do anything I want." "If you hadn't told me to do it, I would've done it."

Herein lies a common, but illusive, source of insecurity. It is possible habitually to expect more from "it" than "it" can produce. Timing plays a significant part in this problem. We tend to want what we want *now*. The demand for an immediate gratification stamps "it" as ungiving and needing to be forced. This unrealistic demand for immediate service not only contradicts the fundamental impression that "it" is generously available to "I," but it also tends to contradict the basic trust in the goodness of life.

As a result of not getting our way, we feel frustrated and angry. Our anger may not be expressed in stamping our feet and screaming oaths, but in a complaining, grumbling, self-pitying attitude. There is a child in most of us who parades himself instantly when we are frustrated or over-tired.

But the complex situation which sponsors the emotional insecurity lies in the unconscious conflict between needing to control our inordinate demands upon "it" so that we do not promote our own frustration. We must keep our expectations both reasonable and realistic. The limits we encounter in a given situation which restrict our gratification stand like mute parents saying "No" to our requests. We resent these limits and this resentment joins with the repressed hostility from childhood when our parents would not let us have our way. The result usually is a negative attitude toward life, a pessimistic viewpoint, a tendency to view life as only a discouraging cyclonic routine of endless frustration. These attitudes are all self-defeating. They find their roots in this second level of development, but they are elaborated by the habitual way we face life situations.

When we grew a little older, perhaps to three or four

years of age, we made a very important discovery, and this opened the way to a third level of development. It was, "I'm like Daddy; Mama is different." Or, "I'm like Mama; Daddy is different." The discovery of sexuality started many changes. First, we began to practice being what we were, a boy or a girl. Second, we began to idealize our parents more and more, first one and then the other. The parent of the same sex became our model of what we were to become in life— a man or a woman, a husband or a wife, a father or a mother. The parent of the opposite sex, by his endorsement in loving approval, reassured us that we were desirable as either a man or a woman, that we could become a good husband or wife, or father or mother. To accomplish this, we desired to feel special to first one idealized parent and then the other. We needed their undivided attention and affection, and we worked to get it.

We didn't realize it at the time, but we employed all the strategies we had learned in the power struggle with our parents to get that "special" feeling. We were at times possessive, sometimes demanding. We sulked and rebelled. Sometimes we felt special because we obeyed and were rewarded with praise. At other times we neglected our duty and felt special because we were irritating. We found a special feeling in the undivided attention we received when our parents were angry with us. As a result of these strategies, some good and others very bad for us, we developed many complexes in our personalities during this period. Among those traits which promote insecurity are deep feelings of inferiority, the need to control our love objects, a fear of being controlled or obligated if loved by someone, fears of being rejected or humiliated. Some of us developed patterns of hiding feelings, concealing opinions, being arrogant and talkative, being withdrawn and a loner, patronizing, etc.

This third level brought a new dimension into awareness. In each level of development, self-esteem is the key issue. In the first, it was, "I have value because I am waited on." In the second level, it was, "I have value because I can do what

I please." In the third we added, "I have value because I feel loved just for me."

Frequently we see adults still looking to be special to someone they regard as an ideal authority figure. They say by their actions, "If you loved me, you would give me your undivided attention. I want to feel special to you." This is a replay of an unfulfilled childhood wish. Some adults still try to be special by being aggravating, but now they have elaborated their abilities by the use of satire and sarcasm. Witty criticism is often used to enhance the feeling of being special.

It is disheartening for any adult to conclude that his value as a person is only because he appears well or performs in an acceptable manner. Some women I have met have the underlying anxiety that if they grow old and lose their attractive appearance, they will be nothing. They will have no value as a person, for all their value is perceived in their beauty. Some men I have met have also an underlying anxiety that if they were unable to earn money and provide for the wants and needs of their family, they would mean nothing. To feel valued only for appearance or performance can be a mighty factor in the problem of emotional insecurity.

Romantic relationships provide a means of feeling special to someone whom you regard as special. Each person idealizes the other extravagantly and enjoys reaffirming and being reaffirmed. Feeling special is verified in the idea of being exclusively privileged. But, because of the nature of romantic relationships, they can be both a source of great security and of intense insecurity. We usually track into our romantic relationships all of the tendencies toward insecurity latent in our personalities.

Origin of hostility

We experience three emotions which are non-relationship feelings. They are hostility, guilt, and fear. Hostility says in effect, "You are bad; I don't want you." Guilt, in effect, says, "I am bad; you don't want me." Fear says, "I am in danger, and I must protect myself." One emotion is a relationship feeling. It is the emotion of giving and receiving love. Love says in effect, "We belong together." Inner security develops in loving relationships; insecurity develops under the influence of hostility, guilt, and fear, for they are non-relationship emotions.

In the first level of development, the child became angry at having to wait for food. He has been hungry and gratified, but there is the waiting period until feeding time. At first he thrashes about, trying to rid himself of his irritations, then he increases his appeal to a very loud, angry crying. It is obvious that he is angry because he refuses to eat. He is so occupied with feelings of anger he has forgotten his hunger. When he does eat after a little coaxing, he may gorge himself. His greed is so great that he would try to eat enough so that he will not suffer hunger again.

We see traces of these feelings in adult life. People tend to resent having to wait for a desired gratification. Then when they get what they want, they don't want it. Jill wanted Gerald to ask her for a date. By the time he noticed her and invited her to go some place with him she was tired of waiting and angry at him. When he did finally ask her, she angrily refused. Some people resent having to wait so much that when they get what they want, they hoard greedily beyond their needs.

In the second level of development, the child becomes angry at not getting his way. He wants what he wants *now*. When refused, he tends to become furious, especially if tired.

A most common evidence of this kind of anger in adult living is seen where we become angry when something is not pleasing to us. It may make no sense to be angry, but we feel angry anyway. The traffic stops on the freeway when we are in a hurry for work. The phone rings and a gabby neighbor wants to talk just when we are frying steaks. A parent is dead tired and Junior awakens in the night with a stomach ache. We schedule "it" to provide what we want, and when "it" doesn't, we become angry.

A very pernicious form of anger arises in this second period. It is called envy. The child is so intent on getting what he wants that it infuriates him to see someone else having it already. In adult thinking it may appear like this: "She plays the piano beautifully. I always wanted to play well. I hate her." "He is a good athlete; I hate him!" Envy is rated as the most destructive form of hostility, for when we envy, in this sense of the word, we despise the very person we should idealize. This leaves us with no way to love that person. Also the resentment blocks our incentive to try to obtain what we really want for ourselves, because we envied it in the other person.

In the third level of development, the child becomes angry at not being served immediately, and at not getting his way, and because he is asked to share his love objects. He becomes jealous when he is not special. This type of hostility is manifested abundantly in adult living in romantic relationships. Jealousy can have a reality reason if the lover is actually untrue, but often jealousy is based upon the fantasy of the lover possibly being untrue.

Hostility is a categorical title for a large assortment of emotions. They all are defensive and projective in nature, and they range in intensity from being irked and irritated to feeling angered and enraged to feeling malicious and hateful.

We have mentioned three forms of hostility because they are fundamental. Greed is a one-object hostility. I am not gratified, and I want all I can get so I will not suffer again.

Envy is a two-object hostility. You represent my ideal and have what I want to possess for myself. The two objects are you and what I want.

Jealousy is a three-object hostility. You are receiving the love I want for myself. The three objects are you, your lover, and me.

There are three primary causes for hostility. One is a feeling of rejection. I want relationship with you, but you refuse me. Another is frustration. I want my plan to work but it won't. I am losing control. A third is humiliation. I want your admiration so I can feel self-esteem, and you belittle me.

All hostility is an attempt for "I" to overpower "it" to get what "I" wants—basically more self-esteem. Hostility is a violation of the dynamic balance which must be maintained between "I" and "it" to hold a steady sense of security. Hostility may be intended by "I" to provide what seems best; instead, it actually destroys much more than it provides.

Beginnings of guilt

Feelings of actual guilt do not begin until the third level of development, but early roots of the dreaded emotion begin in the first level and proceed through the second. When the tiny infant has to contain his anger in order to preserve objects he wants and needs, he begins to feel bad about himself. Mother says, "See! You got angry and broke your little truck. Now it is all broken." Johnnie looks at his broken truck and feels bad. It is broken, and he did it.

This means that the child must learn to contain his anger. Instead of his anger finding an object in "it," the anger turns upon "I" as the object. The child sulks or pouts. This is an early form of what is later called depression. At first such a bad mood doesn't last very long, but if it is permitted to be a manipulative device to get his way, the child will sustain the mood for longer periods of time.

As a child grows and experiences gratifications from "it" and learns to tolerate more and more frustrations, he is able to conform to the wishes and demands of his parents. In other words, he is taking his parents into his mind. It works something like this: the child reaches for some candy and mother stops him and tells him to ask first. The child reaches again, and the mother commands more emphatically, "Ask first!" Finally, perhaps after a few slaps on the hands, the child wants some candy and hesitates. He asks mother, "May I have some candy?" This is how the parent becomes part of the child. The internal parent is called the conscience, or superego.

The child may be willingly obedient, anticipating the wishes of his parents, but it is not until he becomes old enough to struggle with the problems of sexual awareness that his conscience actually functions as an entity in his mind. Before this he was controlled by conditioned reflex, a forerunner of the conscience.

This does not mean that guilt is always related to sexual matters. It does mean that guilt is a social relationship emotion. The child is old enough to be developing his sex role identity, a confidence in his manhood or womanhood. At this time, guilt, shame, and inferiority feelings become a real problem.

Guilt should be a reparative emotion, but it actually is not. Guilt should indicate what is wrong so a person can correct himself. But guilt does not work that way. Guilt not only says that you have done a bad deed, but that you are a bad person. We can correct the bad deed by reforming our conduct, but we cannot overcome the feeling of being a bad person without outside help, a topic which I will discuss in a later chapter.

Guilt and hostility both relate to a loss of self-esteem. When I believe "it" is to blame, I strike out against "it." This is hostility. When I believe I am to blame for the loss, I strike against myself. This is guilt.

Guilt is not only an indication that we have offended "it" by doing something we should not have done, but since parents from "it" have been taken into "I" and become a controlling part as well as a praise-giving part, "I" has nowhere to go for restoration of self-esteem when the conscience condemns. "I" is condemning itself.

Early evidence of fear

Fear is an emotion which is based upon some painful experience. We fear repeating that experience. If a child has not experienced trauma in a particular situation, he will show no fear. A parent can toss his child into the air in various precarious ways and the child shows no fear because he has never been dropped. After he has fallen a few times, he will manifest fear at the possibility of falling again. He isn't very old, however, before he associates one experience with another and manifests fears when he has no apparent reason to be afraid. Then he needs to be solaced by his parents and taught to overcome his unrealistic fears.

Observers tell us that there are three universal fears among children: the fear of being alone, the fear of strangers, and the fear of darkness. Neither of these is based upon an apparent experience, but probably is related to the birth trauma, where he lost the protecting influences of his mother.

Fear can arise from circumstances, problems with "it" which threaten to harm. Fear can also arise from within the mind. Fantasies can produce many fears. Often we become afraid of a bad dream. We imagine ourselves in serious trouble whether we are awake or asleep.

When fear is realistic and helps one to protect himself from harm, fear is a good emotion. But when fear has no specific object, or the basis is unrealistic, then fear is debilitating. It confuses the mind so that the person cannot organize his thinking. It is possible to become so afraid that one is actually paralyzed. Fear distorts values, so that in a fire people save useless articles and allow valuables to burn. Fear distorts the time perspective so that one becomes confused. The mental picture of the event he fears seems to collapse into a blur.

Love is a different emotion

The first experience we had with feeling loved was the tender, attentive, affectionate care of our parents. All through life we tend to interpret love by this early experience. When anyone shows us tender care, or is voluntarily concerned with our comforts, we feel loved.

The second experience we had with feeling loved was when we were allowed to have our own way. Our parents allowed us to do just what we wanted. All through life we tend to feel loved by others when they do not interfere with our functioning autonomously. We feel loved when others respect our right to make our own decisions and carry out our plans.

In the third level of development, we had another fundamental feeling of being loved. We felt loved when our parents gave us undivided attention in an accepting way. Then we felt really special to them. So all through life, we are inclined to feel loved when we are made to feel like a special person.

Love is the good, positive, quieting emotion of happy relationship. Love that is genuine always seeks the welfare of the one loved. Love is redemptive of the bad effects of hostility, guilt, and fear. Love builds a sense of identity and inner security.

4

Understanding Human Relationships

People who are emotionally insecure are almost without exception people who have been deprived of love in childhood.

As soon as we mention love, we must qualify what we mean by the word. Love has a variety of meanings. This has been true for centuries, for love is instinctively desired by everyone and always has been. Anything as desired as love is bound to have counterfeits.

Love, in the way we think of love, is basically a sharing of oneself and a caring for the welfare of the object loved. Conditional love, manipulative love, and other forms of pseudo-love cause as much damage to a growing child's sense of security as does no love at all. Love that isn't all it claims to be sustains insecurity as children become adults.

These love-defective adults naturally express to their children, as well as to the world around them, the same false love they have been receiving. They know no other love. It is this handicap in society that continually promotes emotional insecurity from generation to generation.

51

Why love is so important

Love is a relationship emotion. When we think of relationship, we must bear in mind that it is unnatural for people to be void of relationship with others. Relationship with other people has been the fundamental experience of life for each one of us.

First, we were related intimately to our mother in the prenatal state. We started life as a vital part of our mother. We heard the sounds of her digestion, the rhythmic beat of her heart; we were rocked gently by the swaying motion of her body. As the time of our birth drew nearer, we became more and more aware of the emotions of our mother. When she was frightened or anxious, we became anxious; when she was happy, we were content.

After birth, we were intimately cared for by our mother, and for several years we enjoyed a symbiotic relationship with her. Before birth we were attached to her for the supply of our life needs; after birth we continued to be sustained by her attentive care. She was the source of our security and satisfaction. In the first three years of life, our father served in a mother role. He did not become a male to us until we became aware of our own sexuality. Then we began to relate to him as a father, and we began to relate to the femaleness of our mother. Then after we became adult, our parents held the respected position of parents emeritus, and we continued a relationship with them as adults.

Because we related to our parents, we are able to relate to our siblings and other members of society outside the home. Relationship has been the key to our emotional growth and sense of well-being ever since we were conceived. Love is the relationship emotion.

People who love uphold, protect, and honor each other; they identify with each other's feelings and concern themselves with each other's benefit. "Love worketh no ill to his neighbour" (Rom. 13:10). When a person becomes disillusioned with life and withdraws from personal relationships, he contradicts his fundamental nature; he isolates himself from the source of supply of many of his emotional needs.

The Bible teaches that in the beginning God created man in His own image (Gen. 1:27). We also read that God is love (1 John 4:8). Love is the nature of God. This means that God is a Person who relates to people. He is love. He is the great Lover; we are responders to love; we are in His image. He is not a supreme being only; He is God, a Person who relates to people who respond to His love.

We are related to God though we do not see Him. "No man hath seen God at any time" (John 1:18). We are intimately related to Him because He is sovereign of all, He created all things and He sustains all things (Col. 1:16, 17). "In Him we live, and move, and have our being" (Acts 17:28).

God originally created man in a symbolic uterus, the Garden of Eden (Gen. 2:7-15). Since that original creation of man and woman, God has used the woman's uterus to bring new persons into being. Our original parents were expelled from the Garden into a world of distress; so when we were born, we were cut off from our mother to learn to fend for ourselves in a world of distress.

God has been relating to mankind in love ever since the creation. He has made and kept promises (Deut. 7:8); He has rescued (Ps. 146:8); He has disciplined (Jer. 31:3; Heb. 12:6-8); He has redeemed (John 3:16); He forgives sin (1 John 4:10; Rom. 5:8); He regenerates spiritually (Eph. 2:4, 5); He calls us His children (1 John 3:1).

Relationship is natural to us because we are in God's image. We love because it is our nature to love. Love is syntonic, or compatible to our nature. This means that once we love an object it becomes a permanent part of our being. We can never expel love. The more we express love, the more it grows.

Hostility, guilt, and fear are non-relationship emotions and are dystonic, or not compatible to our nature. This means that these emotions are not permanently a part of us; they can be expelled. Often when we express these emotions, we find relief. We can externalize them and overcome them. This does not mean they will never reappear, for these are reactionary emotions. We can always react again to a new situation with hostility, guilt, or fear, for we have a long-standing habit of reaction.

Since hostility, guilt, and fear are non-relationship emotions, they do erode and seem to destroy the relationship feeling of love. If these negative emotions are dealt with and overcome, love can be restored. The sense of relationship can be restored when the non-relationship feelings are removed.

What is the emotion of love?

Relationship is made possible by a natural talent called "empathy." Empathy is the ability of one person to sense the feelings of another. Feelings are communicated empathically mostly by sound. The sense of sight and touch play a small part in the ability to empathize. To verify what we are saying, I suggest that you turn the volume off on your television and try to grasp the sense of the emotions and moods of the persons presenting the program. This will give you some idea of how dependent upon sound we are for communicating.

By the way, as you watch your television with no sound, you are simulating the world of the deaf. This is how life appears to them. Touch communicates a little, but probably less than sight to empathic communication for the profoundly deaf.

We first understood our parents when we were infants by our ability to empathize. We caught some of the meaning of the words they used by the tones of their voice and the facial expressions. Empathy underlies the ability to learn to speak. As the child watches his parents make certain sounds the feelings they are expressing when they articulate sounds, they begin to shape their mouth similarly and learn to articulate also.

Because of the ability to empathize, the mind is able to identify and to learn. Identification happens because of empathy, and love happens because of identification. Empathy is: "I sense how you feel." Identification is: "I feel as you feel, and I have a sense of feeling as if I were you." Love says: "Because I feel as you feel, and I have a sense of being like you, I enjoy you and am interested in your welfare." It is because of identification that we become like the people we love, for we adopt their ideals and absorb their mannerisms. This is why we say love is the relationship emotion, for love makes us related to each other emotionally in a sharing frame of mind.

When we have feelings of anxiety manifested in either hostility, guilt, or fear reactions, we become self-concerned. This self-concern blocks the use of our natural talent of empathy so that we are insensitive to the feelings of other people, except as they might relate to our hostility, or our guilt, or perhaps to giving a reason for feeling afraid. This self-concern keeps us from identifying with others and consequently from loving them. This is why we label these three negative emotions as non-relationship feelings.

How the love emotion matures

Love grows naturally through stages of development while the child is maturing physically and emotionally. In the first level of development, when the infant is exceedingly dependent, we might logically presume that love feels to him like comfort and pleasure. We would expect the infant to explain his love feelings like this: "I feel loved when mother makes me feel comfortable."

In the second level of development, when the child is running about the house and getting things for himself and the power struggle with his parents is in full bloom, we might imagine him explaining his love feelings like this: "I feel loved when mother makes me comfortable, and I feel loved when she does what I want her to, or she lets me do as I please."

In the third level of development, which begins usually during the third year of life, the child might explain his love feelings as: "I feel loved when mother makes me comfortable, and I feel loved when I get my way, and I feel loved when I feel special, that is, when I have my parents' undivided attention."

Love is cumulative in its development, as we have noticed.

What feels like love at one period of life will always feel like love. So in adulthood, love feelings blend together, and because of other emotional needs relating to responsibility and the desire to give love, they take on the added dimension of sharing and giving. Ideally, when love has reached maturity, one feels loved when someone accepts his love and allows him to share himself.

Thus love should grow full circle: at first love is felt when one is taken care of; at maturity love is felt when one is giving himself to minister to another.

The exchange principle in human relationships

We all started life in the position of dependency, needing to *be* loved. From that first early experience with love and through all three levels of maturation, we needed others to take the initiative to show love to us. Our ability to love others as adults now is derived from the love we have received as children. Fundamental concepts of love are in the receptive position.

This fact is consistent with the truth that we are created in the image of God. God is love. The Bible does not say that God is just loving; it says "God is love" (1 John 4:8). "Love is of God" (1 John 4:7), and "We love him, because he first loved us" (1 John 4:19). When we love, we are exercising an attribute of God. In other words, we are acting out in human emotion a quality which belongs primarily to God. This happens because man is created in God's image and in His likeness.

God is love. He is the Lover. We respond to love. We need to feel loved. We are people who instinctively need relationship for emotional maturity and fulfillment in life. Before we can feel love for others, we need to experience being loved ourselves. Usually this experience is provided in childhood by parents, but for those who have been deprived of love in childhood, love can be experienced initially by relating to other adults who love them, but the resentment over being deprived must be resolved.

Our sense of God's love is rigidly conditioned by our experience of being loved by our parents. If parental love has been conditional, then naturally we expect God's love to be conditional. If our parents have associated overindulgence with love, then it is natural for us to expect God to be overindulgent. If parents were punitive and restrictive, then God is viewed the same way, and the sense of His love is likewise distorted. Though this is true of childhood conditioning, these distorted perceptions of God's love can be modified in adulthood by loving association with friends, and by reading the Bible to discover a clearer understanding of the nature of God.

Since each person is void of the ability to originate love, but only loves as he has experienced being loved, then each person is in a receptive position to *be* loved. Each in a social relationship expects the other to love him, but each also has the ability to show love from his own emotional reserves to ignite or inspire the love responses in the other. This puts love on an exchange principle.

When we meet someone, we say "Hello," and sometimes add, "It's a nice day, isn't it?" The person responds to the attention with a similar greeting, and a conversation of exchanging ideas begins. If the person ignores the greeting, we feel rejected and begin to "drop" him. We write people who write to us; we exchange gifts with those who give; we compliment those who are complimentary.

We can give love *if* we have received love. We can initiate love if we are able to inspire a response. Having received love from another person, we can only accept a certain amount of this quality of attention before we reflexively feel the urge to respond in a loving way.

This exchange pattern is inflexible. Anyone who tries to cheat in the exchange game sooner or later eliminates himself from personal relationships. The old adage, "You can't get something for nothing," certainly applies here. As a simple illustration, think of Christmas and the exchange of greeting cards. There are those who keep lists of names and cross off individuals who did not send a card the previous year. They give a greeting if they have received one, and when they receive a card before they have sent one, they hurry to get one in the mail, or if it is too late for Christmas, they send a New Year's greeting.

We give attention if we have received attention. The quality and price of gifts are often compared to make sure one receives about as much as he has given, or vice versa. The complex tit-for-tat interaction in social relationships is most intriguing.

Sometimes there is a delayed reaction which subtly operates in this exchange game. If Mabel compliments Hazel for her fine cooking, Hazel is not likely to pay her back immediately with, "I like your cooking too." She will hold the praise and pay her debt of gratitude when Mabel is not expecting it. "Your hair is especially nice today," she might say at an opportune moment. There are many conversational strategies in this delayed exchange of compliments which politely conceal the fact that there is an exchange happening. Because of this, each person can profit by the illusion that he is being voluntarily blessed by the other. This voluntary aspect in the exchange greatly enhances the value of the verbal love-gifts.

Perhaps the parent-child relationship is an example of the longest delay in the exchange of love. It appears that the parent's love is totally expendable, that there is no exchange happening until the child reaches adulthood and appears to neglect his parent. Then we may hear the complaint, "After all the love I have shown you, and you treat me this way!" Sometimes parents are more obvious in their expectation that love will be returned. They plainly indicate that since they have cared for the child he must plan to take care of his parents in their old age. The illusive fact in this situation is just this: children who feel loved by their parents have love for their parents and sincerely want to attend to their needs when they are old. They don't want to feel they are paying them back.

The avoidance game in relationships

Our family was driving across country, and in a midwestern town we stopped for some groceries. While my wife was in the store, I sat in the car. Two farmers standing at the street corner caught my eye. They were visiting. I could not hear what they were saying, but I was impressed by their manner. They seemed delighted to meet each other, but neither looked at the other directly. First one would talk, and while he was talking he was surveying the landscape. The other also looked away, but occasionally looked directly at his friend who was talking as though to study him carefully. When it was his turn to speak, he also looked away to some object while his listening friend either looked away or scrutinized him carefully. Their eyes never seemed to meet; they never looked at each other at the same time; yet they seemed very satisfied with their conversation.

I have often thought how well this illustrates the avoidance game we play in relationships. We observe the other person when he is not looking. We avoid getting caught making our observation. We instantly look aside when it seems his eyes might meet ours.

What are we doing? We are relating, but without actually admitting a personal interest. We are imagining that we appear a certain way to our friend, but at the same time we seem afraid to look the other person in the eye to verify the impression we think we are making or to discover how little or how much he may be interested in us. We take no cognizance of the fact that our friend is not paying attention to the image we wish to project, but he is forming his own impressions out of the candid observations he makes when we are not looking. The image we think we might be projecting of ourselves may have very little to do with the impression we are actually giving.

Another avoidance strategy is to focus attention upon an object in a situation instead of directly upon the person we are addressing. It is important to discuss various objects of interest other than one's own feelings or the feelings of the other person, but when we *must* discuss other things, we are avoiding getting close.

Some people find it most difficult to share themselves in a conversation. They have never thought about talking directly.

They have always related to others through the medium of discussing the weather, politics, religion, the children, taxes, and the news. To say, "This is how I feel," or, "My idea about the matter is . . . ," or, "This is where I stand on the subject," may be entirely too personal and revealing to be comfortable. Yet at the same time, these people yearn for closer personal relationships.

Many people communicate freely with each other while avoiding closeness. They tell clever jokes, confirm each other's ideas, show each other favors, but never share their personal feelings. If a crisis occurs, one is bereaved or ill or is in some financial crisis, they might express sympathy or concern, but they would feel awkward doing so.

Meaningful relationships are not only concerned with sharing the latest news, or in commenting on the purchase of a new car or dress; they are relationships in which the people involved are free to be themselves with each other regardless of what feelings they show.

Each person is a combination of strengths and weaknesses. In one's own perception of himself, these two must be kept in balance. If a person views himself only as strong and superior, he will appear arrogant and conceited. If he views himself only as weak or inferior, he will appear timid and unassuming. How we project ourselves in personal relationships is very important, but we must be honest. A person is seen as humble who is able to view himself realistically as both strong and weak, and he does not disturb the balance between the two when he communicates with others.

Positive and negative mental attitudes apply here. The person who habitually thinks positively attracts the love of others by displaying his strengths. He tends to disturb the dynamic balance between strengths and weaknesses by concealing his weaknesses so that his strengths will be more apparent. In his exalted self-esteem, he will expect others to admire him, because he honestly considers himself better than they. He does not return value for value in the exchange game. Naturally he is resented by others because his conceit implies that they are inferior. He is expecting verification of his worth without giving the same in return.

The person who habitually thinks negatively tends to present himself as weak in order to attract the love of others through their sympathetic understanding and generous assistance. He also disturbs the dynamic balance between his sense of strength and weakness by giving emphasis to his shortcomings, inabilities, and failures, and concealing from himself the value of what he has achieved or might accomplish. If he gave value to his actual abilities, he would have to acknowledge his strengths and be more positive and more responsible.

Because he is unaware of his excellencies, and his pattern is to think negatively, he cannot give value to others. He tends only to be aware of his weaknesses, so this biases him toward cheating in the love exchange, though he is unaware of what he is doing. He expects others to give to him when he considers himself unable to be of value to them in his present condition. He is something like the pauper who begs at the door. No matter how much you give him, he will only come back for more.

People tend to avoid the negative person. Consequently, a person who assumes a negative attitude in life tends to eliminate himself from the very resources he needs for self-verification in social relationships yet he blames others for the problem.

In various ways we avoid personal relationships, and each is self-defeating. Avoidance is a way of being unrealistic. When we avoid we are giving in to our fears and staying just as insecure as we have always been.

Problems in relating to others

1. *Determining reality.* Each person wants and needs loving relationships with other people. But each has to *give* a little love in order to *get* a little love, and each person has an unsatisfied need to receive. This puts everyone at a slight disadvantage in relationships, especially if he is so in need of love that he is emotionally insecure. In his anxious state

of mind, he must receive love before he can give love, for he has no emotional resources. To do this he is likely to feign love when he really does not feel it, and resent having to do so, which tends to increase his superficiality in order to recover his resentment.

Pretending to be interested in others when there is basically no reality to the interest is very common in social interchange. Each person seems to know that the other is not as genuinely interested as he seems to be, but in these pseudo-attitudes many are being hurt. No one wants to be deceived, and so nearly everyone is careful to protect himself from being so involved that he might get hurt. Some people love genuinely and feel rejected because their love object did not trust them to be genuine. Some take advantage of those who trust.

Not only does each person have difficulty deciphering the other person's true expression of himself, but he has a problem being absolutely certain he is in touch with all of his own feelings. He may feel that he is openly representing himself to another person, and then discover later that he did not feel as deeply as he thought he did at the time.

Dating is a good example of this kind of problem. A lover can be carried away by the immediate mood of the situation and commit himself to the other person beyond his actual desire for responsibility. If both felt the same, it would not be much of a problem, but usually one person accepts the commitment of the other only to find that it had no depth.

2. *Mutual self-verification.* Some people are more certain of their identity than others, but all appreciate being verified by the praise or attention of a friend. The problem lies in the fact that each needs verification because of a lack of emotional development in childhood, but neither has the parental authority over the other to make the validation stick.

Jane says, "I feel so inferior. I can't do anything right." This may be a sincere remark, but when her friend, Margaret, tries to reassure her, she can't accept what Margaret says as having value. Margaret may say, "I don't see why you should feel inferior. Why, you can do so many things well. I wish I could do some of the things you can do." Jane remains confused. "I know you feel that way, but I still feel inferior no matter what you say I can do." Margaret could never take the place of Jane's parents to give her the assurance she is seeking. In fact, Margaret admitted to being inferior to Jane, so how could she have the authority to help her? This makes the situation something like the hungry trying to feed the starving.

3. *Confusion in identity.* This is a common problem in social relationships. We confuse marks of identification with true identity. Every person has an appearance. He looks a certain way, and he varies his appearance somewhat by the way he dresses, but how he appears is not an actual identity factor. We tend to rate people by how they appear. "He looks nice; he can be trusted." "He's a mighty fine person," we say, and all we really know about him is that he dresses attractively. "She's beautiful," or "My, how sloppy! I can't imagine anyone liking that person." All the "fat" person needs to do is reduce, or the dowdy person to sharpen up, and we feel attracted to him and give him a different rating. Appearance reveals how a person feels about himself, and it has some bearing upon how he feels about those he is with. But appearance is only a mark of identification. It is not identity. It distinguishes one person from another; it does not actually say anything about the character of that person.

Performance is another way of rating people, but performance is not anything more than a mark of identification. "He's a doctor"; "She's on television every day"; "He's a ditch-digger"; "She has two earned doctorates and three masters degrees." These are marks of identification acquired as a result of hard work, but they should not rate a person as having more value than another hard worker who is known as a "common laborer." Even the person who does little or nothing should be treated with respect, for he is a person too. Performance ratings are only marks of distinction between individuals. Performance has no right to use identity value to make one person feel better or worse than another.

A third mark of identification that brings confusion in our thinking is social status. Social status is closely related to appearance and performance, but it also has a hereditary factor. Society is stratified into levels of social importance, and each is a reflection of society's opinion. Color of skin, wealth, class, and sometimes religion and political views have a way of rating a person in our social structure. The slogan, "All men are created equal," is speaking to actual value, to identity. Social inequalities tend to depreciate some and exalt others. We inherit a tendency to be a "respector of persons" and often confuse the person with the office he holds. The President is still a person just like the rest of us, and it is helpful to keep this in mind.

Appearance, performance, and status are three areas of confusion in our identity values. We use these values to attract attention and love, but we tend to exceed the true value of these three and give them a place in our sense of identity to reflect personal worth. Because we make this mistake about others in our evaluation of them, we also make the same mistake about ourselves. This confusion puts us in a futile position of always trying to improve our sense of personal worth by upgrading our appearance, or our performance, or our social status. This confusion multiplies our insecurity.

4. *Parental components.* Our fundamental relationships have been with our parents, for they nurtured us at the beginning of our lives and taught us what to expect in relating to other people. We depended upon them for guidance, advice, correction, for doing things for us we couldn't do for ourselves. We interacted with them and discovered how to be independent of them for what we could do for ourselves. We tried to be special to them to discover our true worth as a person.

Many of these very basic experiences in childhood have been frustrated, deficient, and incomplete. Our parents had emotional needs of their own and were unable to minister adequately to ours. Theoretically, if we had received the parental love we needed to meet our basic needs, we would not have this sense of incompleteness and unwholeness which is so disturbing to our adult life.

Now that we are adults, we unconsciously compensate for

these deficiencies. We become attached to certain people who impress us, and we make a big issue of their excellencies. In doing this, we tend to idealize them and respect their judgment beyond their ability to function or their desire to be involved with us. Sometimes we select someone who needs to feel this sort of importance, and this person becomes attached to us. He has a need to dominate, and our need to depend upon him and exalt him meets his emotional need to control and to be liked for it.

It is not harmful to honor others and to be respectful of their excellencies, or to admire their achievements and fine qualities. The harm begins with awarding them parental components of authority to control. We don't think of them as parents, or usually make this association, but if we analyze our attitudes, we find that we are interacting with these people on certain occasions as though they were authority figures with jurisdiction over us to govern us or to award us for our virtues. We maneuver to get their praise or counsel or help in some way. We want their special attention. If we are unable to obtain the desired response, we tend to feel rejected or humiliated. Often we will feel angry, and without a rational reason we might want to hurt them or reject them.

Self-consciousness is a manifestation of this problem. We are uncertain of what impression we might project to others, and we feel embarrassed or timid or self-conscious. When we feel self-conscious, we are being unrealistic in our feelings about others. We may realize that we are unnatural and unrealistic, but this doesn't usually help to overcome the problem.

Some people seem to worship the great god "They." They are always wondering what others will be thinking of them. "What will *they* be thinking?" is a nagging preoccupation. We can rationalize, "What difference does it make what they think? It is likely that they are not thinking of us anyway." But this doesn't stop the problem.

Parental components are a fundamental source of difficulty in most marriage problems. One partner exercises a parental authority over the other, or one tends to behave like a child before the other. These parent-child feelings greatly disturb the romantic desires in marriage. There is a natural incestual barrier in each of us. Parent-child feelings blot out the normal sexual attraction that each has for the other. So the marriage becomes a defensive, hostile power struggle similar to the infantile power struggle between parent and young child, but often is much worse and more frustrating. The romantic fulfillment in marriage is entirely dependent upon maintaining a simple peer feeling between the partners. When parent-child feelings occur, the inequality arouses anger and demolishes romantic desire.

Parental components in social relationship distort and disturb the interaction. Sometimes this is manifested in being dependent for advice or help when one could decide for himself or help himself. It is not uncommon for people to use this dependency to build a relationship and not realize that they are creating a sick, self-defeating situation.

Parental components are sometimes manifested in people being domineering and demanding. It is as if the two-year-old child in them were still seeking limits, but never accepting the limits others keep giving. This makes them ready to assume a parental role, and they do not realize that they are actually looking for others to stop them and limit their sense of authority to the areas of life for which they are responsible. In other words, people keep telling them to mind their own business, but they never hear the suggested limits.

We not only tend to control others, but we seek to be controlled. We unnecessarily involve ourselves with others to feel indebted to them, or we may maneuver to get them to feel indebted to us. In this way we are trying to make our relationship with them more secure, but, of course, it never works that way.

We subtly entice praise and adulation from others. We need their admiration to support our own self-esteem. We do not realize that when we do this we are also vulnerable to their criticism. We have made people our judges. We have awarded them a parental component. When we stop to think about it, it is surprising how these illusive parental components permeate most human relationships.

5. *Hypersensitivity to criticism.* The reason for this reaction is not easy for the person himself to discern. A person who is hypersensitive to criticism usually has an image of himself that is most deficient. He often expresses this feeling by saying, "I sometimes feel like I'm nothing. I'm not only inferior, I'm nothing." No one can bear to feel that he is nothing or that he is inferior, so he sets about to prove to himself that he is not "nothing," that he is not inferior. He tries to be exceptional in appearance or in performance in order to prove he is not "nothing." Everything is all right until someone finds fault with him. The criticism reminds him of being nothing, and he has a terrible sense of failure. All his efforts have been in vain. They have discovered his deficiency.

The perfectionist is a victim of this syndrome. He is trying to be perfect to prove to himself that he is not a total zero. He is trying to be so perfect that it will be impossible for anyone to discover a fault. If this should ever happen, and it never can, he will probably be convinced that he is something. He can never be perfect enough to prove to himself that he is not nothing because he honestly believes that he is nothing. He is denying this idea, and by perfect behavior he is expecting to fool himself.

Summary

We all need relationships to feel fulfilled in life. Love is the relationship emotion. We learn to love and to accept love from our parents during our childhood years. Each person needs to be loved to verify his own identity, and this mutual need makes everyone subject to an exchange principle in relationships, each giving to the other in order to get what he wants. We avoid getting hurt in relationships by various styles and strategies of communication. These avoidance maneuvers give personal relationships a pretense factor which makes it difficult to feel secure in the expression of love. We tend to confuse our appearance and performance and social status with our true sense of identity, and this adds many difficult problems to social relationships. Parental components bring many unrealistic values into relationships and cause much confusion. When we try to prove to ourselves and to others that we are something we are not, we make ourselves vulnerable to criticism and to praise in excess of the real value of these evaluations.

In all of these problems in social relationships, we find a common factor of self-centered concern. Each person is functioning more or less from a sense of initial prerogative in the situation, and each is trying to achieve something for himself. This creates a vacuum in relationships which needs to be filled, but the usual social situation has nothing to fill this need.

5

Let the Boss Be Boss

Our abilities and resources are limited. Our knowledge, skill, wisdom, and time are also limited. We know this, but on a feeling level we sometimes function as though we had no limitations. We tend to expect too much of ourselves and of situations.

Kenneth waited until the night before his mid-term exam to prepare. He reasoned as the days passed, "I can handle it. I always work better under pressure." When he started to work, he found he had much more to do than he could possibly get done. He stayed up all night studying, then nearly fell asleep during the test. His low performance was not a result of his lack of ability, but of expecting too much from himself in too short a time.

Hilda was discontent with her appearance. She spent many hours each day grooming herself. It seemed that she could never look the way she wanted. She could not duplicate her mental image of how she wished to appear.

Elmer interrupted his conversation with me every few minutes to do a little ritual of touching his wrist and jerking his head four times. I finally asked why he did this. At first he did not want to tell me, but he indicated it was to keep his family safe. "There are four in my family, my wife and I and two children," he explained. "Whenever I hear the word 'four' or any multiple of that number, I have to do this little ritual to keep them safe from harm. I know it sounds peculiar, but I just have to do it. I know something bad would happen to them if I didn't, and it would be my fault."

Elmer had feelings of omnipotence related to his movements, and so he went through certain movements to save his family. Hilda had a gloriously omnipotent image of herself in fantasy which she could not reproduce in reality, so she was dissatisfied with herself. Kenneth had a sense of omnipotence in his ability to study and he disregarded the element of time as an important reality.

There are many forms of omnipotent thinking. Each is a remnant of childhood memories which still affect the thinking. Omnipotence in one form or another is present in all types of emotional insecurity. People expect something of themselves which they cannot produce, and because of unrealistic expectations they cannot maintain a healthy sense of self-esteem.

Omnipotence is a term used more properly of God alone, for He is almighty. Omnipotence means all-powerful in an absolute sense. It is used psychologically of human behavior when people assume an all-powerful or an all-knowing attitude.

There was a period of time normally in every person's childhood when his unharnessed imagination gave him feelings of omnipotence. He imagined he could fly high in the sky, or leap over mountains, or swim through ocean storms, or run so fast no one could see him. Such fantasies are a normal part of growing up. Usually this period does not last long, but for some it lingers on into adulthood in certain limited forms.

We enjoy seeing cartoon characters doing unusual feats, defying the laws of gravity, disregarding time and human endurance. This is because we all have fundamental memories of experiencing omnipotent fantasies. These cartoon characters still capture our imagination, but now they seem ridiculously humorous.

It is not the unusual manifestations of omnipotent thinking that deserve our attention just now, but the everyday feelings of omnipotence we consider to be normal. Feelings of omnipotence are related to self-esteem. Early in life we all had a pleasurable experience in feeling omnipotent. It was such a glorious experience that we want to return to it, but we can't. As we approach this grandiose feeling about ourselves, we enjoy self-esteem. When we lose that good feeling, we experience a loss of self-esteem..

The origins of self-esteem

A newly born infant has not yet formed the sense of being a person. He has not identified his mother or father as actual objects. He has an undefined feeling about everything. He is only cognizant of what is pleasant and what is unpleasant. About the only experience he has had from which he can interpret his new world is the security he felt being rocked by mother's movements and held securely in his prenatal home. The sounds of his mother's body functions came to his ears as a humming sound. After birth he is comforted by being held securely and rocked gently, and he is comforted more by a humming sound than by any other.

The newly born infant has not learned to distinguish between what is "I" and what is "it" (see Chapter 3). He is, according to whatever awareness he may have, a part of everything and the world is a part of him. When he feels miserable, he cries and allows the world to flow into him and restore his tranquillity. He experiences a glorious omnipotence at this time which he will never again be able to attain. This grandiose feeling of excellence leaves a fundamental memory toward which he will always try to return.

As time passes, the infant experiences more and more dissatisfactions and frustrations. He continually faces new situations he cannot master. These frustrations and their resulting tensions cause him to differentiate between what is "I" and what is "it." His nursing relieves tension; so do his body movements, restoring tranquil, omnipotent pleasure associated with taking something into the mouth, and with body movements.

From very early in life, the infant attributes pleasure to the mouth and to swallowing. Everything that is pleasant is incorporated as part of "I." Everything that is unpleasant is spit out and rejected as belonging to "it." This is why anger, which develops very early, is a negative emotion. The infant emphatically spits out whatever is unpleasant. His need to defend against being invaded by unpleasantness increases, resulting in anger.

We have explained hostility as an emotion which is not compatible to the self. It can be spit out and externalized. This is because anger is related to irritation. Love, on the other hand, is compatible with the self, for it is associated with pleasantness. It cannot be externalized and moved away from like hostility.

Self-esteem is self-love—that good feeling of worth which a person has when his inner sense of satisfaction approaches the memories of omnipotence he once had during the first days of life. These memories he has forgotten as specific experiences, but they abide as fundamental desires. The original, reflexive sense of omnipotence which is lost from awareness as an actual experience lays the foundation for self-esteem. We are always desiring and gravitating toward a feeling of self-love which feels very comfortable. Anything which causes us to feel less omnipotent lowers our self-esteem, and we tend impulsively to react negatively to retrieve that loss.

As a child continues to develop, things happen which produce other feelings. He not only strikes out against "it" in anger when frustrated, but he begins to identify with his mother, who is the main source of his frustration as well as the source of satisfaction. The frustration caused by mother is not in this context regarded as a bad thing but a good thing, for frustration comes in the normal process of waiting for the bottle to warm . . . not getting to be held as long as wanted . . . or waiting for mealtime. Identification is a defense against unpleasant tension.

Identification is a mental process based upon the natural ability to empathize. As the child senses his mother's feelings empathically, he begins to feel as his mother feels. This ability to feel as another person feels, or feeling as if one is actually the other person, is called identification. Since the child identifies with his mother, he takes his mother into himself psychologically. He thinks and acts like her. She becomes an object within his mind.

For instance, the mother is delighted with her baby. This affectionate delight communicates empathically to the baby to make him delighted with himself. He gives value to himself by virtue of the feelings of value his parents give to him. Also, when the parents correct him, his identification with the parent makes him begin to correct himself. The command, "You cannot have candy before dinner," can unconsciously block the child from demanding candy when he sees some just before dinner.

One very important factor in development is that the child's identification with his mother neutralizes his natural coercive rage against her for not always giving him just what he wants. As he senses that she has his welfare in mind, and disobedience can bring him harm, he cancels his rage and adopts his mother's attitudes as his own.

When the child is about eight months to one year, the mother progresses in the child's perception of her from being a part-object (like hands, face, arms) to a whole person. By the time he has had his third birthday, he is beginning to identify with his father as a male for the first time. Previously, father served as a whiskered version of mother. Boys identify with fathers to develop manhood. Girls identify with mothers to develop womanhood. Boys normally practice being like their fathers to capture the loving admiration of their mothers, which verifies their manhood. Girls normally practice being like their mothers to capture the loving admiration of their fathers, which verifies their womanhood.

Identification is a mental mimicry in which the child perceives himself not only to be like his parent, but at times actually to have his parent's characteristics, as though he were the person of his parent. As the parent lovingly restricts and instructs him, he feels as if he is the person of his own parent and begins to restrict himself. To the degree the parent punishes him, he tends to punish himself in the absence of the parent. As the parent compliments and rewards him, so the child congratulates himself for doing what pleases the parent. He tends to think as his parents and to talk as they talk. He not only identifies with their strengths but also with their weaknesses and faults. This is how the parent is internalized and becomes a significant factor in the conscience, for good and for bad.

In normal living the parent naturally will frustrate the child in the processes of controlling him and teaching him to control himself. Thus the child is forced to acknowledge the omnipotence of his parent and to accept the fact that he himself is not omnipotent. Ordinarily this is beneficial, for the omnipotent parent is internalized by the process of identification, which strengthens the conscience, or superego, with concepts of absolute right and wrong.

Ideally, a child internalizes a loving, omnipotent parent, and as a result, displays good self-control and becomes well disciplined. Instead of having to have his own way and be independent of authority in order to feel omnipotent, he develops to a level where he chooses to conform to authority, and he prides himself in being right. By identifying with omnipotent authority, he has an internal parent who gratifies him with feelings of self-esteem for being right. The emotionally mature person feels good about himself when he is right, and he feels a loss of self-esteem (guilt) when wrong. He has become his own parent by the process of identification.

A child feels a sense of omnipotence, or self-esteem, when he identifies with someone he regards highly. The child does this naturally. "That's my Dad!" Or, "I want you to meet *my* Mom." In either case the child is feeling omnipotent by being associated with someone he idealizes. As adults, we also do this. "I shook the hand of the President," we may hear; or, "I used to know Senator Goldbrick personally," or, "There are several ministers in our family tree." The person making such a statement is feeling a little greater because he is associated with someone of social rank. He has raised his level of self-esteem by association.

It is necessary for a child to pass through the hero-worshiping stage to develop emotional maturity. By identifying with the hero, he shows the potential of heroism himself. Then his feelings of self-esteem come from his growth toward accomplishing those ideals he has formed.

Also, the child receives self-esteem from the tokens of love he receives from adults. He gains self-esteem when he is treated with acceptance and affection, and he loses self-esteem when he is rejected and humiliated. It is the promise of gaining self-esteem and the threat of losing it that motivates a child to obey authority and to develop introspection and self-discipline.

Guilt feelings are to be understood as the internal parent of the superego, scolding, shaming, or punishing the ego. The person condemns himself: "I know I did wrongly. I am bad." This is guilt. His superego withholds esteem from the ego as a parent would withhold praise and punish the child with shame when he did something wrong. These values are reinforced by various experiences one has during life.

Sexual drives are intimately involved with feelings of self-esteem and omnipotence. We speak of a man having confidence in his manhood, or a woman in her femininity. Any maiming of the body or loss of body function immediately implies a loss of self-esteem in relation to the sexual function. Many young women are concerned about being inadequate sexually because they do not possess certain body measurements of bust, waist, and hip. Sexual gratification in marriage for both sexes is a tremendous source of self-esteem, and a lack of it can also be a devastating threat to self-esteem.

The process of growth which involves daily coping with delays, frustrations, tensions, rejections, and humiliations produces an enormous change in feelings of omnipotence and self-esteem. The person as a child felt omnipotent when all was pleasurable and delightful to him. After coping with all the trials and vicissitudes of growing to adulthood, the person finds his sense of omnipotence from obedience to his own ideals, goals, and values. At first he felt omnipotent as part of the omnipotent world; as a mature adult he became omnipotent by internalizing the omnipotent world and identifying with it.

Deterrents to self-esteem

The basic problem with emotional development is that no one has ever had perfect parents with whom to identify. We have identified with parents who have not been ideal, not always loving, with emotional problems of their own. While they may have wanted the best for us, they taught us their own anxieties and inadequate ways of coping with problems. They were angry with us and did not love us at times when we should have been guided in love. Their restrictions were not always motivated for our good, but to meet their own needs. Some of us have been corrected improperly by parents just to please an interfering grandparent, relative, or neighbor. Some of us have not been corrected when we should have been or we have been punished unfairly. Others of us have felt more rejected by our childhood corrections than loved. We have not internalized the kind of parents we needed to develop a good, realistic superego.

No one is perfect. We tend to react to our children as our parents reacted to us when we were small. Parents often tell of impulsively reacting to their children's mischief in the same unreasonable and unrealistic way that their parents did when they were small. Though they vowed such a thing would never happen, it did, and they feel helpless to make much of a change.

Lona came to my office recently, seeking advice. Her fifteen-year-old daughter was beginning to date boys, and she was worried. Lona declared, "My mother used to be suspicious of me when I was a teen-ager, afraid I was not as moral as I should be. It used to bug me terribly. I swore that if I ever had a daughter, I'd be understanding and talk things out with her and not accuse, but I'm doing just what my mother did to me. I don't know how to stop it." Lona had to outgrow the bad influence of her mother.

Another very important factor which has injured our self-esteem in adulthood is that many of us defied our parents' authority when we were children. We did what we could to get around their rules. Often we were angry at them, whether permitted to declare our hostility openly or not. We sought self-esteem from being independent of our parents instead of aligning ourselves with them. This has affected our conscience so that now as adults we tend to defy our own good judgment. If we are on a diet, for instance, we reason that just a little piece of cake will not hurt. If we know we need to stop smoking or drinking, we tend to resent even the restrictions we place upon ourselves. We arc defying the internal parent now as we used to defy our parents when we were young. Instead of finding self-esteem from doing right and being right, we find some measure of gratification from being able to get by with something questionable.

Procrastination might be a good illustration of defying the inner parent. We know we must write a letter, pay a bill, do the dishes, mow the lawn. We plan to do it, but we have difficulty getting to the task. It is easy to put it off because something else seems more important at the moment, or we are just not in the mood. We are actually perpetuating the power struggle of childhood with our parents, only we can't win because our parents are represented by the sense of duty we have toward our task. We are defying our own better judgment and punishing ourselves with self-criticism.

A child who does not receive love from his parents according to his need may find a false self-esteem in being able to outsmart them by becoming independent of their controls. His parents may have corrected and threatened him in anger; now as an adult he is unconsciously acting out revenge. His original anger toward his parents destroyed any idealization he might have for them. Now, as a result, he finds his self-esteem coming from acting out revenge, in defiance of social custom, advice of others, opinions of authority figures, or statements of civil law.

This is part of the reason why some people resist the idea of believing in God or becoming a Christian. They know that God is holy, that He is almighty, and that He knows all things. Since their parents occupied at one time in their lives the position of omnipotence to reward and to punish, and they were not always consistent, but sometimes most rejecting, they assume that God is like their parents or worse. They have achieved a certain resource of self-esteem in their pattern of living by doing as they please whether it is absolutely the right thing or not. They have gathered other people around them who think and act much the same as they. Instinctively, they know they will have to give up this practice if they trust themselves to God, so they feel they will lose greatly by becoming Christians.

Often people think: "If I could only erase the idea of God, then basically moral law would become a fable, and I could do as I please." It is natural to want to throw off all moral restraints and to indulge in whatever one desires, but life is more complex than that. The battle against the voice of conscience is a futile one indeed, for defiance of ideals always leads to self-depreciating feelings. We cannot feel fulfilled unless we feel whole, and we cannot be whole when we contradict our own good judgment.

Need for changing parents

We have observed how the child grows from infancy to adulthood and how his conscience is formed by parental influences. The illusive factor in the process of maturing is that we expect to outgrow the need for parents. "Someday," we reason, "I will not need my parents, and I will be an adult who is totally self-determining." No one ever outgrows the need for a parent, as we will soon see. Such thinking is unrealistic and self-defeating; it is rebellion against authority.

We have come to realize that we all lack superego development in some degree. No one has had perfect parents, and no one is able perfectly to obey his own good judgment. Instead of giving in to our desire to be independent of parental influences, we should think of bringing our conscience into a more perfect state of development by taking the Biblical view of growing up. Our natural tendency is to think of ourselves as so mature by the time we have reached adulthood that we will be totally self-determining and self-sufficient. But life does not bring us to such an adulthood. The Biblical point of view is that parents are intended to prepare the individual to relate to God and to have a parent-child relationship with Him.

Parents in God's great scheme of things are to serve much the same as a booster stage does to a rocket nosecone. As the booster thrusts the nosecone into a predetermined orbit, so the parents prepare their children to orbit as adults with the will of God as their center of gravity. Parents, according to the Bible, should never think of themselves as owning their children as personal possessions, but rather as being granted a stewardship of them until they can relate to God for themselves in the varying situations of life.

God is the author of life; He is life. God is sovereign in His universe. Not only did He create all things, but He is the One who manages all things and holds all things together (Col. 1:16, 17). He is eternal, and He says that "Every one of us shall give account of himself to God" (Rom. 14:12). He has "appointed a day, in the which he will judge the world in righteousness" (Acts 17:31). But He loves each one of us (John 3:16), He has communicated Himself to us (Heb. 1:1, 2), and He is "not willing that any should perish, but that all should come to repentance" (2 Pet. 3:9). We can trust in God and find Him to be real and personal. He can become to each of us just what He is, our Heavenly Father!

When we do relate to God in the Biblical way, we "cleanse our conscience" from various corruptions (Heb. 9:14; 10:22). We establish a relationship with the perfect Parent through His grace in Jesus Christ. Believers have a way of overcoming the bad influences of earthly, fallible parents and the influence of others that has not been good.

Life is three-dimensional

When we only think of ourselves, we are living a mono-dimensional existence. Such a life is autistic and entirely self-containing, most unfulfilling.

When we relate to other people and practice the love-exchange pattern of interaction, we find life to be more fulfilling and interesting. As we have noticed in Chapter 4, the exchange pattern of relating to others does not provide a means of preventing the three negative emotional reactions—hostility, guilt, and fear—from injuring our happiness. We are living in a two-dimensional structure of life: "I" and "it."

When we function on the love-exchange principle, we must channel our hostility, but we must be careful that it doesn't cause us to lose relationships we value. We must avoid our guilt feelings, and in chapter 3 we listed several ways we usually employ to dodge the feelings of guilt. We must be as courageous as possible in facing our fears. We do not wish to manifest weakness in coping with our problems. Two-dimensional living provides no adequate resolution of these three negative, defensive feelings which do harm to our self-esteem and feelings of identity.

When a person will come to God by the only way that God will accept—faith in Jesus Christ as his own personal savior from sin (John 3:36; Acts 4:12)—he starts in motion a fourth level of development and a new resource for security and self-esteem. He brings a third dimension into his life.

You will recall that the first three levels of development happen early in childhood. The first is dependency, then autonomy, then sociability as we became sexually aware of being either a boy or a girl. Each of these three levels evolved involuntarily simply by virtue of our development. This fourth level is a voluntary level of growth; it is spiritual and based upon a voluntary commitment to God.

The first three levels of development left us insecure and deficient in our resources for self-esteem, the problem being that the omnipotence is not completely in the superego because our parents were fallible and not really omnipotent. We are still, at least in part, searching for self-esteem as we did before we developed a superego, that is, by the pleasure of immediate gratification. When we open our minds to God and trust Him to accept us as His own children (Eph. 1:6), we immediately find a new life, a new security, a new self-esteem. "If any man be in Christ, he is a new creature: the old things passed away; behold, new things have come. Now all things are from God, who reconciled us to Himself through Christ" (1 Cor. 5:17, 18 R.S.V.).

It would be impossible to explain all that happens at spiritual conversion, but we can see how receiving Jesus Christ is receiving new life. "He that hath the Son hath life; and he that hath not the Son of God hath not life" (1 John 5:12). He is life. He is holy. He is perfect. He is God, and, most wonderful of all, He is love! (1 John 4:8-11). When we give ourselves to Him, we no longer belong to ourselves, but to Him (1 Cor. 6:18, 20). Our sense of being His own possession, His child, gives to Him the power to pronounce us not guilty because of the atonement of Jesus Christ (1 John 1:9-2:1). The penalty for our own godlessness, our sin, has been paid by the Judge Himself! We are saved by faith in Him.

Because of Christ, God becomes our Heavenly Father (Rom. 8:14-17). This father-child relationship with God is kept vivid in our awareness as we read the Bible. This relationship is declared to be sustained by God because He loves us with an "everlasting love" (Jer. 31:3 and Rom. 8:31-39). It is not a variable based upon our feelings about God, but upon His eternal Word and immutable promises (Heb. 6:16-20). So we have a stable Parent who loves us with a constant love and who is available to us in prayer (Luke 11:9-13).

When we experience spiritual conversion, we enter into a personal relationship with God which corrects the problem of omnipotence within our psyche. We stop belonging to ourselves and we start belonging to God. We have yielded the essential right to our own omnipotence, and we have accepted God as our omnipotent One. Because of this commitment, we can experience a freedom from guilt (Rom. 8:1) by His forgiveness. We may not always be able to obey our conscience (Rom. 7:14-25), but we can continue to be forgiven and cleansed as His children (1 John 1:9) the instant we confess our sin to Him. When we trust God to forgive, we find that He restores our self-esteem which our guilt destroyed.

There is no question about God owning everything, for He is the Creator. He also owns every person, for He died for our sins in Jesus Christ's atoning death. The commitment of ourselves that we made to God when we were spiritually converted brought to our awareness a new sense of His ownership. His ownership and His possession of us becomes exceedingly personal. This sense of His ownership and personal concern make it possible to resolve the guilt problem we once had which we were only able to handle by rationalization, intellectualization, denial, and other means.

We are not our own. The One who owns us has pronounced us "not guilty." We could not resolve guilt before because we held ourselves entirely accountable to ourselves and to what others thought. Now, by faith in His justifiication, we are free to feel entirely clean from all sin and guilt. "There is, therefore, now no condemnation to those who are in Christ Jesus, who walk not after the flesh, but after the Spirit" (Rom. 8:1). The walk after the flesh is a self-centered walk wherein we retain the omnipotence and the sense of self-ownership. The walk after the spirit is a God-centered walk where we have forwarded our sense of omnipotence to God and accepted His ownership of us and His possession of us by His "Spirit which He has given us" (1 John 3:24. See also Rom. 8:9).

Let us stop a moment to think what faith in God is. Biblically there is no difference between believing in God, having faith in God, and trusting God. These terms all present the same idea. It is impossible to have faith without trusting something. Faith must have an object. Faith means trusting things, people, self, or God. Faith, or trust, or belief all speak of depending upon something more powerful than self, more omnipotent. It is more than being persuaded, it is a reliance, a committal. To believe in oneself is actually an inner-psyche transaction. We are trusting that we will be able to manage enough inner unity to control adequately whatever is anticipated. It is the ego reassuring the superego that it is capable of controlling the instinctive drives or of managing the situation, or both. The ego is attempting to hold on to a sense of omnipotence.

If I say I believe in God and do not rely upon Him, I am only giving an intellectual assent to Him. I still retain the essential omnipotence. My praying to Him, or worship of Him, will be actually a device to get Him on my side to serve my interests. Since I know who God is, I seek to employ Him in the service of reinforcing my omnipotence and bolstering my self-esteem. I will tend to use His promises against Him to persuade Him to obey my desires and grant my requests. I have not really humbled myself to God, yet I may have given intellectual commitment to the Christian doctrine as I understand it.

If I believe in God only intellectually, I still belong to me and function with the same sense of prerogative in life I have always used. My format for thinking has not changed; I have only attempted to add the almighty power of God to the service of my interests. But when I actually trust God in my sense of weakness to be my sustainer, trust God in my despair to be my hope, trust God in my sense of futility to bring meaning and sense into living, trust God in my guilt and utter sense of nothingness and badness to be my Redeemer, "to forgive me and to cleanse me from all unrighteousness," I have surrendered my sense of prerogative to life, my essential omnipotence. I regard God as my omnipotent One by His grace.

With merely intellectual faith, I may feel sorry for my sins and seek His forgiveness, but only because I wish to escape His wrath and punishment, that is, eternal hell! I am motivated by fear. Whenever I am motivated by fear to yield to my earthly parent or some authority figure, I do not actually surrender. I cannot feel a sense of being "with" the one I am essentially afraid of; I must sustain my own identity and protect myself. The same applies to faith in God. If I am essentially motivated by fear to seek His forgiveness, I am not seeking to be joined to Him, to be identified with Him as His own child. I am seeking His forgiveness so I will not have to face the penalty for my willfulness.

Faith in God is a true humbling before God and it surrenders the natural sense of prerogative in life. It acknowledges the fact of God's wrath against sinners, but it also acknowledges the justice of that wrath. Under fear motivation, God appears somewhat unfair and not absolutely good. Under love motivation, God appears absolutely fair and just and good in His punishment of sin, and I acknowledge my guilt and accept His gracious forgiveness through the atoning work of Jesus Christ.

This is the essential meaning of Romans 6:1-15. We do not have to yield to a tyrannical, demanding God who is determined to punish sinners and who demands a quality of righteous conduct that we cannot obey. Instead, this passage indicates that God has demonstrated His love for us (Rom. 5:8) by paying the penalty of death for sin Himself in the person of Christ. He must demand punishment of death for sinners because of His justice, but His love demands that He give the sinner a chance to live by redeeming him and offering him life.

He died and He has risen; it is all finished. I do not have to give up and die, as it were, to believe in Him. I simply respond to His love as I acknowledge that He has died for me because He loved me. In the person of Christ, I, the sinner, am on that cross, dead! But I, the sinner, am also in Christ alive from the dead to live a new life, a life in union with God. By faith born of love, not fear, "I am crucified with Christ: Nevertheless I live; yet not I, but Christ liveth in me: and the life which I now live in the flesh I live by the faith of the Son of God, who loved me, and gave himself for me" (Gal. 2:20).

If God just forgave me in an excusing sort of way, "You are repentant, so I forgive," I could not resolve my fear of God's wrath. My omnipotence would still be in competition with His, and we would soon clash again. I would have to keep coming continually to seek His forgiveness out of fear. He would be impersonal to me. But God does not forgive in an excusing sort of way. God loves me and does not want me to suffer His wrath, so God demonstrates His goodness in punishing Himself in the Person of His Son on Calvary for me. He died so I will not have to die for my sins. I, by faith, respond to His love by loving Him (1 John 4:15-19).

My loving Him forwards to Him all my omnipotence. I am His. I seek to belong to Him who has loved me beyond my comprehension. I seek His forgiveness, not to escape His wrath as much as to obtain His holiness and find His peace. I want Him!

In doing this, I find a whole new sense of personal worth. I am worth something as a Christian, not because I have done something of value, but because I have identified with Him who is the perfect One. I am a partaker of His divine nature (2 Pet. 1:4; Col. 3:10). He is holy; He is perfect; He is worth everything to God for He is the Son of God. By faith in His Word, I claim to be potentially all that He is—not quantitatively, but qualitatively.

It is one thing to accept the fact of Christ's atonement intellectually and quite another to accept a restored personal worth by identifying with our loving Redeemer! When we can, then we are spiritually raised from death to walk with Him in newness of life (Rom. 6:4). The guilt problem is erased by faith in Jesus Christ. I have a new self-esteem.

It is natural to ask, "But what about sinning after one is spiritually converted?" God has dealt with that problem. Romans 6:1, 12-18 indicates that we have a new motivation and a new life; we have no license to sin because of a ready forgiveness. If we have truly identified with Christ, have felt ourselves on the cross with Him for our sin, we cannot enjoy sinning the same as before. "No one who is born of God practices sin, because his seed abides in him, and he cannot sin, because he is born of God" (1 John 3:9 R.S.V.). It is contrary to the very nature of the Christian to enjoy offending Christ as previously (Eph. 4:30). When we discover that we have sinned, we confess this action to God as a child to his father and find restoration of fellowship (1 John 1:6-2:6). The relationship with God as a member of His family is maintained by the living Christ through His intercessory work in heaven (Jude 24). Fellowship with Him is blighted by the sense of being wrong. The knowledge of the sinful deed reminds us that we have returned to the life we once abandoned at the cross. We have returned to the "weak and beggarly elements (Gal. 4:9); we have repossessed our sense of prerogative in life and our omnipotence. We have not acted in faith.

Faith in Christ provides an answer to the problem of hostility as well as of guilt. When we accept His sovereignty, we accept His ownership of all things, including ourselves. He is sovereign over our situation as well as over our minds. We trust God never to forsake us. That does not mean that God will keep us from pain or misery or death. It means that we have a hope in Him that extends beyond this life to eternity. The injustices we find here will be equalized at the Day of Judgment (Luke 18:7, 8). If we suffer with Him here, we shall reign with Him there (1 Tim. 2:12). In accepting His sovereign lordship of all things, we accept His lordship of us and all that may happen to us. "All things work together for good to them that love God..." (Rom. 8:28). God is in complete control of all that happens to His children or He could not make this statement: "No temptation has overtaken you but such as is common to man; and God is faithful, who will not allow you to be tempted beyond what you are able; but with the temptation will provide the way of escape also, that you may be able to endure it" (1 Cor. 10:13 RSV). He is with us who are His regardless of the trial; He will not let us fall away, but He will make a way for us to endure.

Our hostility functions on the basis of our sense of prerogative to whatever we want as though we owned all things. Our faith in God surrenders that sense of prerogative to Him so that we are willing to accept the vicissitudes of life without resentment over the unpleasant. Ordinarily, we want everything to be pleasant and we tend to resent anything that we don't like. Our faith in God and identification with the sufferings of Christ have taught us that life here cannot provide everything pleasant. Hardship can be beneficial, for in it we can grow more mature spiritually and emotionally. We know He suffered for us, and if He chooses to allow hardship, we can suffer for Him and do so as an expression of love.

Hardships in the lives of adults who trust in the Lord serve about the same function as the parental frustration of children which is intended to teach the child obedience. In Hebrews 12:6-15, God describes His Fatherly care of His children and of their reactions as parallel to the parent-child situations in the home.

You recall there are three types of situations to which we impulsively react with hostility—rejection, frustration, and humiliation. If we feel rejected by someone after we are Christians, we can remind ourselves that He was rejected for us when He died on Calvary and that somehow He has allowed us to be rejected in this situation. It will help us to emulate His love in spite of our feeling rejected on a human level. If we feel frustrated because our plan or schedule for a situation did not work out, we can trust Him for grace to rearrange our plans to incorporate the change. The virtue of patience is being able to accept delay or change without anger, but it takes a commitment to God's loving sovereignty to do it. If we should be humiliated by some mistake we made or by some criticism of others, we can concentrate on the lesson to be learned. We can remind ourselves of our true worth in Christ and out of a sense of gratitude to Him view our humiliation more objectively.

Faith in God places the omnipotence in God and awards Him the prerogative in life that causes hostility. Before spiritual conversion, we can only control or repress or channel our hostilities. We lacked the third dimension in our thinking, the God dimension. Now we can keep from repressing hostility by facing it before God. We choose to be hostile, but we don't have to make that choice. There is a better way. We can return to His sovereign control and return to our love for Him and discover a new perspective in the situation that is not hostile.

Faith in God also brings relief to our fear problems. We are feeling alone when we feel afraid and are unable to identify. We become very self-centered in our thinking. Trusting in God requires a certain amount of identification with God. We are identifying with God when we feel He is strong and that He cares and that He is active in the situation. Fear and anxiety make God unreal to our awareness; all we can think of is the danger.

We must guard against trying to cope with our fears by feeling guilty as though we were not acting in faith. This only complicates our fear problem, for we feel less capable of coping with our fear if we are also feeling less a person at the same time. Nowhere in the Bible does God issue a law that indicates that it is sinful to be afraid. We are not breaking a law when we feel fearful, so we are not sinning. We are not acting in faith, that is true, but God is patient about that. He often said, "O ye of little faith" (Matt. 8:26; 14:31), but never in a condemning manner. He simply reminded them that because He was present they had no reason to fear. This truth is our comfort also in our fears. David said, "I sought the LORD, and he heard me, and delivered me from all my fears" (Ps. 34:4). The Lord reassured His people through Isaiah, "Fear thou not; for I am with thee: be not dismayed; for I am thy God: I will strengthen thee; yea, I will help thee; yea, I will uphold thee with the right hand of my righteousness" (Isa. 41:10). We are not alone when we trust in God, and if we seek the Lord when we are afraid, we can find strength.

Letting God be boss in me gives me the ability by faith to meet life situations without hostility, or guilt, or fear. If I do react with these negative emotions, I can resolve their domination of my mind and accomplish a better way of coping. By faith I have arrived at a satisfying sense of self-esteem (Rom. 12:3). My resources for my sense of worth are more objectively positioned in truth that is written in the Bible. My faith in God is a result of believing what the Bible says (Rom. 10:17). It is not subjective, wishful thinking, or a result of complying with a religious ritual.

By letting the Boss be my boss, I have potentially resolved my omnipotence problem. I have discovered a completely new life, a life based upon fellowship with the omnipotent One. I have found a solid sense of inner security. It's a fourth level of emotional and spiritual maturation. "As ye have therefore received Christ Jesus the Lord, so walk ye in him: rooted and built up in him, and stablished in the faith . . . for in him dwelleth all of the fulness of the Godhead bodily. And ye are complete in him, which is the head of all principality and power" (Col. 2:6-10).

6

Rearrange Your Priorities

A person's priorities determine his center of love, and the center of his love is his preoccupation.

It is normal to be hitched to some focus of interest in life. Those who have lost their goals wander aimlessly and accomplish little. They also enjoy little sense of fulfillment.

Some goals are immediate, others are distant. Goals are related both to basic needs and to flights of imagination. If I am hungry and tired, I have an immediate goal of getting home where I can eat and rest. If I am single, I may have a long-range goal of finding a mate, establishing a home, and having children. If I am married, my immediate goal may be to keep ahead of the avalanche of bills that pour in every month. My long-range goals may be to provide a college education for my children, pay off the house mortgage, and have financial security in my old age. Goals may vary as life progresses, but whether they are immediate or distant they help to organize the use of time and energy. They give direction to living, a sense of purpose, and increased fulfillment when they are accomplished. In order to accomplish our goals, we have to establish certain priorities.

We all have them. The college student who would achieve good grades takes time for study. His priorities force him to discipline his use of time. Priorities force him to give up certain things he would otherwise do. The athlete programs his eating, his sleeping, and his exercise to reach maximum strength. His goal sets up priorities which determine his choices. Priorities are what we put first.

To improve his feelings of security, a person must rearrange his priorities. If he expects things just to fall into place without patient self-discipline, he will be disappointed, for they won't. We can't turn our backs on our problems and expect them to disappear. The carpenter who would remodel his house does not wait for the pile of lumber delivered by the lumber yard to fall into place. He doesn't just expect his project to get done somehow. Instead, he carefully fits pieces together, removes certain walls and builds new ones, repairs damaged areas, and follows a design. So it is with developing inner security. It pays to set up some sensible priorities.

Start with a definite decision

It is not a simple, easy project to remodel one's own personality, but it is possible to make many sensible, enduring adjustments which improve one's feelings of inner security. Whatever is done must be started with a specific decision to do what is necessary and to stay with it until a solution is reached and a stable adjustment is made.

Usually therapy that yields results requires working with a good therapist on a person-to-person basis for an extended period of time. This is because real therapy means more than just learning new facts. It means re-establishing broken relationships and gaining new resources for self-esteem. A person can read books, listen to helpful lectures, and gain many valuable insights about himself. Nothing of lasting value will be realized, however, unless he makes full use of the insights he gains in improving his relationships.

Insight loosens the dominion of past memories upon present thought and behavior. There is an immediate value felt when the insight is first received, but it must be put to work in daily experience or it is lost. Insight alone will not change very much in the personality. When an insight is gained, it is good to tell a friend. Think it through and try to apply it wherever you can. Expect yourself to think or do differently in some small way because of the insight.

As an example, Jenefer wondered why she could never feel ambitious about doing her dishes after a meal. It usually took two or three refillings of the dishpan with hot water and suds before she finally accomplished the boring job. As soon as she filled the pan with water she would think of something else to do, phone calls to make, television programs to watch. Her insight was that she could not attend to her dishes with interest because unconsciously she was still quarreling with her mother about her household chores. When she was a girl at home she dillydallied with her work, and her mother would complain, nag, and threaten by the hour.

Insight alone could not solve Jenefer's problem. She had to go to the dishpan and claim the work as her own, not her mother's. She told herself that mother would *not* be whining if she got busy and finished them immediately. As she worked with her basic insight, she got in touch with anger feelings toward her mother she had buried years before in her unconscious. As she dealt with the anger over her mother's nagging, she found a new feeling begin to emerge about her daily duty of washing dishes. Doing the dishes became a challenge instead of a drudgery. After a while, and with persistent self-discipline, Jenefer reported that it only took a few minutes to do the dishes. There really weren't very many dishes anyway—just what it takes to feed two people, herself and her husband!

Jenefer had to start with a decision to change. Then she was willing to work at the goal until she accomplished the change she wanted. The dishwashing problem received priority value.

Some people mistakenly wish for a miracle to relieve them of an emotional problem. They would like to find a way to grow up instantly so they would not need to work at correcting whatever is wrong. I do not believe there is a miracle cure for immaturity. There are no pills we can take, no springs we can bathe in, and I find no example in the Bible among all the wonderful miracles recorded there where God miraculously short-circuited his ordained processes of growth and maturation. On the other hand, there are many promises of reward to the overcomer. (See Rev. 2:7, 11, 17, 26; 3:5, 12, 21; 21:7.)

The experience of overcoming problems builds character. If we were to be suddenly relieved of an emotional problem, we would soon be in another of a similar nature, because we would not have grown mature enough to handle life on the higher plane. Jenefer could not really use a miracle, though she might have wished for one—at least to do her dishes. She had to work with her understanding of her problem, and as she did, more insight was gained. Then she got in touch with her infantile rage against her mother which was the problem-making emotion blocking her ambition. The hostility she once felt had undercut her normal use of iniative to take hold of her dishes and do them. If she did the dishes, her mother would win and she would feel as though she lost. If she did not do the dishes, she would win, but the dishes had to be done. She would finally get to them, but with many guilt feelings and much reluctance.

Jenefer might have stopped short of total victory, but she persevered. She wrestled with her longstanding attitude toward her mother and resolved her defiance. Now she is a more whole person. She has matured and is more prepared to face other stresses of adult living.

Does Jenefer's story seem trivial to you? Most every person's emotional problem seems inconsequential to the person who does not have a similar problem. It would have been easy to tell Jenefer just to do the dishes and quit the monkey business, but remember, she would have if she had been able! Now she can.

Are you aware of insecure feelings? Do you want relief? Then start with a decision to change, no matter what. Own up to your faults and believe you can overcome them. It might be good to take a pad and write your problem out in detail as much as you understand it. This will help you to organize your thinking and it may prepare you for your first valuable insight. It is very important that you make note of your strengths as well as your weaknesses. It is easy to become so preoccupied with what's wrong with your self that you live a problem-centered life.

Life is not only overcoming deficiencies, it is also occupying what you have overcome. Life is composed of periods of rest and happiness as well as periods of stress and misery. Try to keep in touch with both sides of life. Try to be sensible and balanced about your zeal to improve; above all, be patient with yourself. Growth is always very slow. Sudden changes usually do not last.

Omnipotence is an underlying problem

Most insecure people quickly resent any situation that contradicts their wishful thinking or expectations. They seem to endure life instead of enjoying it. They may show their resentment by a complaining attitude, a critical spirit, being bored, or by self-pity and self-condemnation as though they were not worthy of anything better. Their resentment over what they don't like continually biases their minds against accepting whatever fulfillment is available.

In order to live happily and with fulfillment, life must be accepted as having both pleasant experiences and painful happenings, desirable and undesirable, good and bad. The immature person either expects too much or too little. He idealizes situations and expects everything to be perfect, or he depreciates situations by expecting nothing good. If good does happen, he will usually complain that it won't last.

If we do not maintain a sense of balance between what the situation forces us to accept and what we want from the situation, we can become ill-tempered. We will either be angry continually because we can't get our way, or we will be pitying ourselves because we are forced to live without getting what we want.

The problem lies in the subtle sense of omnipotence within the insecure person's attitude. He is continually forming unrealistic expectations, and this causes situations to appear to fail for him. Each failure should point to his unrealistic expectations, but instead it verifies his reason for being angry and dissatisfied with life.

His expectations are related to his earliest infantile experiences of being served by his mother to his complete satisfaction. Now he is grown, and his life-needs are much more elaborate and complicated, but he is still fundamentally expecting "it" to anticipate his wishes and grant them, simply because he wished.

His resentment over being disappointed, perhaps at first because he had to wait for his milk longer than he thought he could, has developed into a coercive rage. He has learned through the years not to express this rage directly, but simply to complain, to be critical, to be sarcastic, or to turn the rage upon himself and feel sorry for himself because others have all the fun, or condemn himself because he is not worthy of nice things. Reactive depression is often the coercive rage related to disappointment turned in on the self because an anticipation was not realized. The depressed person is not actually feeling angry, but seems to be saying by his attitude, "I'll punish you by feeling so bad myself you can't stand it."

On an unconscious level, the infantile rage is still controlling the insecure adult, and what he doesn't realize is that the rage is robbing him of the capacity to enjoy anything. His pleasures are only momentary. As soon as pleasure continues, he unconsciously begins to defend against the happy feeling. He becomes anxious with such thoughts as, "It won't last," or, "This shouldn't be happening to me, I don't deserve it."

It works this way: when a person is angry because he is not getting his way, and it seems to him that nothing much ever goes his way, that "That's the way life is," he develops a view of the world, the "it," as not caring, not cooperative, inconsiderate, always against him. This attitude is often transferred to God, and God is viewed as unloving, unkind, not good, sadistically enjoying the sufferings of mankind, always holding out the promise of blessing, but really it isn't there. God seems to be creating more problems every day. The person has to take care of himself in a hostile environment, and he is often afraid of life, afraid of the unexpected completely annihilating him.

What the person doesn't realize, and it would be helpful insight for him if he could do so, is that this paranoid attitude subtly robs him of the ability to accept pleasure, for if he should be pleased, he would only be submitting to the ploy of the enemy to increase his suffering when that pleasure ceased. That is why we often hear, "It won't last." They are afraid of intensifying their misery by accepting pleasure, for they are aware of expecting any pleasure to continue. They know that circumstances change from the immediately gratifying to the dissatisfying and problematic. They defend against the unpleasant by avoiding the pleasure of the pleasant.

Love and relationships that fulfill are out of reach for the insecure person until he deals with this subtle core of omnipotence within himself that demands service from others. Whatever relationships they have, and often insecure people are gregarious, are friendships that use people selfishly. Social intrigue is very involved with this kind of motivation, yet we usually do not stop to think of our motives. Our true motivation stands out like a ghost on Hallowe'en, however, when someone does a generous deed or shows us sincere love, and we impulsively remark, "I wonder what he wants from me? No one ever does anything good unless he is looking for some pay." What we are really saying is, "I never do good for others unless I feel I will receive something good in return, perhaps more than I gave."

Thus the insecure person promotes his aloneness. He may be gregarious or he may have withdrawn into himself, but in either case his own omnipotent attitude of being the center of things robs him of relationships that fulfill. He must deal with his infantile dependency and the coercive rage that accompanies it in order to grow toward emotional maturity.

Where the omnipotence belongs

Omnipotence is an attribute of God. He is the only One who is almighty. Our use of omnipotence is only related to our unrealistic imagination and expectations. In our attitudes we assume the role of God in life situations. We are not God and do not have the power to shape situations according to our wishes just by wishing. We are created in the image of God and possibly feel somewhat as God feels regarding a sense of independent self-determining prerogative, but we are not actually God—only an image. We cannot verify such feelings. When we demand that life situations comply with our wishful thinking, we only promote our own insecurity and sense of failure, and maintain our reason for being angry at life and dissatisfied.

When we acknowledge no supreme authority in our life, no God, we try to be our own boss on a primary level. We manage our lives as though we owned ourselves and only gave an accounting to ourselves. We tend to assume a sense of independent prerogative and place ourselves at a serious disadvantage in any life situation. We are unwittingly asking the situation to gratify us on a primary level as though we were the reason for the situation happening.

We are oblivious to the fact that other people in the situation have as much right as we to demand that we serve their wishful thinking, whether they tell us their expectations or not. This obviously leads to unexpected contradiction of interests and to serious clashes of will.

There are also certain physical factors in a situation which are beyond our control. For instance, it rains the very moment we planned a picnic. We shop for groceries and have to wait in a long line at the check stand. Perhaps, to add to our frustration, just as we approach the check stand the cash register jams, runs out of paper, or it is the operator's time to close the stand for a break. There are aggravations in life, and many of them are more upsetting than they need be because of our scheduling of what we can't control. We tend to become angry over these unforeseen factors instead of being more realistic and flexible in our expectations. Our emotional reaction does not make the situation any better, and when we have cooled off, we still have to cope with the matter on a realistic level.

There is a natural omnipotence which resides in the unforseeable and in the unpredictable factors of life. If we learn to cope with these inherent omnipotent factors without an emotional overreaction, we have grown more mature. When this happens, we will be functioning better and be more able to make the best of what we did not want to happen.

For instance, it does not help to curse the automobile salesman who sold you a lemon just because the motor stalled in traffic and refused to start. It is now your car, and if you want it to run properly, you must find a mechanic who can fix it. Your emotional reaction does absolutely nothing about solving the problem.

Another more subtle example of resentment over frustration is Mrs. Foster, who was serving family friends a delicious and elaborate meal. In her haste to serve everything hot, she overlooked the peas and they boiled dry and scorched. This was very upsetting, but her audible reaction was, "I can't cook. I never do anything right. That's my last package of peas!" Mrs. Foster's anger, expressed as self-condemnation, ruined her pleasure in the whole occasion. If she were able to cope better with the unexpected, she might simply have informed her guests that the peas had burned, but that they probably would never miss them anyway, and then proceeded to enjoy the meal.

We all have to learn how to cope with the inherent omnipotence in life situations if we are to mature. A basic rule might be: *Only attempt to control what you are directly able to be responsible for. Only accept responsibility for what you can control. If there is no specific responsibility, there should be no sense of prerogative.*

Actually, the inherent omnipotence in a situation is a manifestation of God's sovereign control of all things. He has the right to allow any happening that in His gracious providence He chooses. He is not only our own personal God and personal Sovereign, but He is the God of all that is "it" or "they" in any situation.

I do not presume to suggest that God is deliberately frustrating people, as some seem to feel, but I believe He has the right to frustrate us if in His wisdom that would be good for us. It would be good for us if our frustrations could teach us that He is good and that He loves us personally. This would contradict our basic attitude that life itself is bad, and it is only good if we are able to get things going our way. I believe He allows us to cause our own frustrations so that we can learn to align ourselves better with His great scheme of things, letting Him be God. He is graciously speaking to our minds by our encounter with the frustrating and disappointing things that happen in order to forward our unhealthy sense of omnipotence to Him, that is, our sense of independent prerogative. He wants to be our God, and He has every right, for He is God and He loves us and expressed that love at Calvary in Jesus Christ His Son.

In Hebrews 12:5-11, God describes Himself in the role of father dealing with us who believe as His children. He emphasizes that He loves us, regardless of what may be happening to us that is hard to bear. He says He is like earthly parents in that He must use frustration, sometimes pain, to teach us lessons that we otherwise would not learn. Earthly parents know that a little pain applied properly in the right place will change the will of a stubborn child from one of defiance to obedience. And the child will not be obeying out of fear but love, because he feels secure in the parent's enforcement of his word.

In this passage God likens himself to the earthly parent who uses pain or unhappy circumstances for the benefit of His children. If we have an omnipotence problem, seeking our way stubbornly, then it is loving of God to allow us to suffer the consequences of our error so that we will turn over our omnipotence to Him and find our security in Him.

Instead of realizing that God is at work in the lives of every one of His children, speaking to them through the omnipotent factors in life situations, we, His children, tend to resent Him as if He were an omnipotent tyrant who is totally uncooperative and unsympathetic with our needs. We tend to confuse God with the feelings we had about our own parents when we were disciplined by them. In a very significant way, we Christians tend to continue the unfinished power struggle we had with our parents in childhood when we try to "walk with the Lord" in faith. We find ourselves attempting to manipulate God in devious ways. One is to use His gracious promises against Him; "Lord, you promised; now I expect you to answer this prayer," instead of reminding ourselves of His promise to encourage our faith, and realizing that, "if we ask any thing according to his will, he heareth us" (1 John 5:14). But we resent Him for not answering our prayer as we did our parents for not granting what we wanted, and we doubt His love as we did our parents'. Another common attitude toward God derived from childhood is, "He answers other people's prayers, but not mine. God has favorites. "You pray for me. I think He will answer your prayer quicker than mine."

Omnipotence is a stubborn factor in our personality. It is easier to think about it and to talk about it than it is to let go of it. Truly, when you stop to think about the matter, the act of trusting God is an act of letting Him be God, letting Him have the omnipotence. If we walk by faith, as we are often told to do in Scripture, we live a life with omnipotence where it belongs—in God.

When we give God the omnipotence, we award Him prior claim to all that pertains to our life. This is a very important truth.

Christians say they belong to God, but they have a hard time living as though they do. Children know they belong to their parents until they are of age, but they often think and behave otherwise. As we have just noticed, the way we related to our earthly parents definitely affects how we relate to God when we become Christian, but we change that as we "grow in grace, and in knowledge of our Lord and Saviour Jesus Christ (2 Pet. 3:18).

There are three infantile needs which interfere with true

commitment to Christ, and because of this, block our apprehending the security we might find in our relationship with Him. Jesus discusses them in Luke 9:57-62. One is the persistent desire to have luxurious surroundings with many conveniences. One willing volunteer for discipleship met with Jesus' words, "Foxes have holes, and birds of the air have nests; but the Son of man hath not where to lay his head." Jesus confronted him with the decision that faces every person who would be Christian. Are you willing to put obedience to Christ ahead of physical ease and pleasure—the luxurious conveniences of life? Is He first, really first? To the degree we are able readily to answer sincerely, "Yes" (and unconditionally), to that degree does God have our omnipotence, and to that degree do we love Him. I believe this is the message of this passage.

The second potential worker met with another problem exposing his infantile drives. It is the drive to be well-pleasing to parents, a drive which keeps us subject to their authority to some measure. "Suffer me first to go bury my father," was his request. He was putting his natural responsibility to his father ahead of his responsibility to Christ, and Christ rebuked him and gave other orders. Sometimes God may choose to use us in other lands, other circumstance. He must be our central authority figure.

The third man volunteered his services, but he asked to bid farewell to his family first. Again, Christ rebuked. Only God can be first. If any other person or group of people have first place in the heart, God does not have the God place—the omnipotence. The affections of earthly family relationships are right and proper and ordained of God, but they must not replace our affection for God. "Love the Lord thy God with all thy heart..." (Mark 12:30). "He that loveth father or mother more than me is not worthy of me: and he that loveth son or daughter more than me is not worthy of me" (Matt. 10:37).

There is one prerequisite to living the Christian life, and that is simply that Christ shall be *first*. He must have the priority. He asks that kind of love from us. In this passage

He cuts through our three human weaknesses, our three hang-overs from childhood. He must be first ahead of physical pleasure; He must be first in our relationship to authority figures; and He must be first in our affections. "If ye then be risen with Christ, seek those things which are above, where Christ sitteth on the right hand of God. Set your affection on things above, not on things on the earth" (Col. 3:1, 2).

A decision to give Christ a prior claim to our inclination to physical ease and luxurious comforts cancels the domination of any immaturities we may be having which stem back to our first level of development as infants. The tendency to pamper ourselves with physical pleasures will not control us as long as we sincerely put Him first. We can then accept hardship without resentment, but with a measure of thanksgiving. A decision to put Christ first as our sovereign Authority in life cancels our tendency to expect to manage our own lives. This decision will nullify the unresolved power struggle with authority figures from our second level of development as a child. A decision to put Christ first ahead of family affections helps us to be free to serve Him with a single heart. If Christ is truly first in our affection, we will not be so concerned about what others think of us when we feel we must do something a little unusual in obedience to Christ. We will be overcoming a hangup from our third level of development and be less plagued by feelings of rejection and inferiority.

As we are able to accept unchangeable factors, the unexpected and the unpredictable, the painful and the distressing, as evidences of His gracious beckoning—"Come unto me, all ye that labour and are heavy laden, and I will give you rest" (Matt. 11:28)—then we are walking by faith. We will have forwarded to God our right to be self-determining and omnipotent and will be growing emotionally and spiritually and becoming more realistic in our attitudes. God will be acknowledged as real and actively companioning with us in the circumstances of life. We will be opening the way for life to be truly fulfilling and rendering eternal benefits. We will thus accept the sovereignty of God in our lives and at the same time be accepting our responsibilities, our privileges, and the trials which so easily reveal our weaknesses as manifestations of His will.

Self-esteem may be derived in two ways

Self-esteem, you will recall from Chapter 5, is a feeling that is vital to a sense of emotional well-being. When we were very small, in our first month or so of life, we experienced a state of grandiose omnipotence related to complete, restful gratification that we never forgot. Though we do not remember the experience as a specific memory, yet we keep trying to recapture that wonderful omnipotent feeling. The degree to which we approach that good feeling about ourselves we call self-esteem.

Self-esteem can be derived in two ways. One source is an immediate gratification of some sort. "I feel good." "I have finished the project and I feel good about it." "I just met an old friend and we had the nicest visit." We may have just had a good meal or a brisk walk and we experience a feeling of inner delight. Another source of self-esteem is the internal parent of the conscience. "The checker made a mistake and gave me too much change. I could have kept it and she'd never know, but I didn't. I feel good about myself. I have done the right thing." We congratulate ourselves when we have done something well or have been right. We can also lose self-esteem by criticizing ourselves for being wrong, by blaming ourselves.

We love God and identify with Him, the omnipotent One. We feel right and good because we have identified ourselves with God. This is a good and safe omnipotence. It can only happen as we place Him first. He must have the priority in us. As we have said, by letting God be my boss, I open the way to purify my conscience of the bad identifications I have made with human parents and authority figures.

The problem is that we can find self-esteem in two different ways. One way is through *getting our own way* in a situation. We desired a sensual pleasure and we got it. We worked hard to accomplish something praiseworthy, and we bluff our way in life, or we can be passive and entice others *is right,* obeying conscience. "I am a good person—I did what was right." This way to self-esteem may involve resisting temptation to obtain a sensual pleasure because it would be wrong. It may be a result of working hard and never being noticed, but enjoying the satisfaction that someone else is benefited, perhaps as an act of our love. "I love my family and sacrifice for them."

One source of self-esteem often conflicts with the other. One says, "Get what you want regardless of rules or restrictions"; the other says to do only what is right. One is related to the childhood desire to get what we wanted regardless of our parents. The other is related to obeying them and finding their praise.

Much insecurity results from this inner conflict of motives. The conflict occurs for several reasons. One is that when we were children we were able to skirt our parents' authority so that some of their control of us was only relative to whether they could catch us or not. Another is that our parents did not always discipline us in love, but sometimes in anger. We felt the rejection of their insults and unfair punishment more than we felt we had done wrong. So we developed feelings of rebellion to their authority over us. Now when our conscience speaks up, we unconsciously rebel and usually rationalize to give ourselves some reason to do it anyway. A third reason why conscience is in conflict with the desires is the general breakdown in the relationship with our parents when we were small. We were more or less on our own, and what our parents didn't know didn't seem to matter.

Nevertheless, when we do act out against our conscience to take advantage of some opportunity for gratifying a desire, especially if it is something sexual, we tend to regret the incident and blame ourselves after it happened. Our conscience attacks us after it is too late instead of preventing the evil from happening. It is as though we had found a delightful thing and enjoyed it, then suddenly our internal parent caught us in the act, or after the act was completed, and punished us.

When we truly let "the Boss" be our boss, we reorient

our whole process of thinking (Rom. 12:1, 2). We are good by virtue of being united to Him, not primarily by virtue of getting just what we want, by accomplishing something worthy of praise, or by receiving admiration from others we have pleased. When we truly love the Boss and He is first, we love Him so much we want to be perfectly aligned with His will. We read His Word to understand Him better and to know His will because we want to be right in His eyes. (See Col. 1:9-12.) This attitude begins to resolve our inner conflicts and heal the insecurity within us. As a result, new feelings of inner security emerge. We have surrendered our independent prerogative to Him, our self-determining omnipotence. We are then free from the motive to act in contradiction to our conscience. This, in essence, gives us a cleansed conscience (Heb. 9:14). We are motivated to be like Him, to please Him, to glorify Him. We would not want to grieve Him (Eph. 4:30). When we love God enough to care about His grief over our sin, we are not likely to be motivated to rebel and to sin.

When we have done something pleasing to God, and we know it, we receive an exceedingly wonderful sense of self-esteem. We are not only good by identifying with Him, but we are good because we know we have obeyed the leading of His Holy Spirit. There is an immediate sense of God breaking through the veil and making contact with us in a moment of time, giving us a sense of His reality. Many will testify to a sense of absolute reality in this experience which words cannot describe.

Priorities determine sources of self-esteem

From the Christian's point of view, there are also two sources of self-esteem. One is his old, unconverted resource, and the other is his new, spiritual resource. One is "me first," and the other is "God first."

The first source is not secure, for there are many variables which cannot be resolved. One variable is our ability to do as we please. Sometimes we are more successful in getting our way than at other times. We can at times be aggressive and bluff our way in life, or we can be passive and entice others to serve our wishes. Another variable is our perception of how others really think of us. We do many things to get them to like us, then we wonder if their response is genuine. We manipulate and so lose the appreciation of their actual feelings. Furthermore, they want admiration from us, as we do from them so they are likely to please us to make us admire them. Then there is the conscience variable. Sometimes we may feel quite proud of ourselves, and then again, the same thing may happen and we might just take it for granted, or even feel guilty. Our internal world is not as stable as we would like to think.

The second source of self-esteem—faith in God through the Lord Jesus Christ—is stable. The only variable is our own ability to release our sense of independent prerogative to Him. God is absolute, and His Word is permanent. When we find our self-esteem in our relationship with God, we are moving toward a more stable sense of inner security. We may feel insecure at times, but as we relate to the Absolute, the permanent One, we feel secure in Him. In the sense of His omnipotent providential care, we restore unity within ourselves.

The Bible does not teach that we have a once-for-all sense of inner security as a result of faith in God. Our feelings are variable, for they are reactions to situations. God is constant, we are variable. We may feel very stable and secure today, but tomorrow, with a different set of circumstances, we must continue to choose to exercise faith in Him. By so doing we grow. We do not climb up on a plateau of unchanging inner stability just because we believe in God. We have an unchanging position with Him as His children—that relationship is secured by God's promises (John 10:28; Eph. 1:13, 14; Heb. 6:14-20; Jude 24, 25). The sense of that relationship, the feeling of His nearness, or the reality of His presence varies from day to day according to our attitudes. We are commanded to "Let the peace of God rule in your hearts" (Col. 3:15). The verse itself implies that we may have times when we do not have peace, but that it can be restored if we return to God. "Draw nigh to God, and he will draw nigh to you" (James 4:8).

We always have a choice; we can come to God and love Him or we can refuse. Love must be voluntary or it is not love. There is only one relationship with God that the Bible speaks about as the life, and that is a love relationship. Love that is love must be voluntary. God loves us voluntarily; we must love Him voluntarily. This leaves us at the point of a constant choice to *keep* God first. As we keep God first, we hold on to security, a solid, stable sense of self-esteem. This is how it works: Remember, our lack of self-esteem is a result of conflict within our psyche as well as a result of conflict with the environment.

Let us consider our inner conflict from the standpoint of Biblical truth. We read that "God is one" (Deut. 6:4; Mark 12:29). All of God's attributes are in perfect harmony; there is no fragmentation within the nature of God. He is absolute; He is one. His sovereignty and truth and justice are never in conflict with his love and grace and mercy. He always wills what He foreknows is good, for He is holy and good.

Man was created in God's image to glorify Him. God is invisible and infinite. Man is visible, tangible, and finite. God is the Person; man is a personality reflecting God's attributes in his nature. Man's purpose in life is to glorify God (1 Cor. 6:20). We are in God's image to reveal His nature in a specific, tangible way. As He is truth, so we must be truthful; as He is just, so we must be fair and honest; as He is love, so we aspire to love expendably and unconditionally as our ideal in relationships.

Since all God's attributes are in perfect harmony, it is innate in man's nature to be one unified whole. Man craves to feel a sense of inner unity. Disunity and fragmentation within the psyche are enemies to the mind of man. Many forms of mental illness are characterized by fragmentation of the mental processes. Inner security is a mental state in which there is unity and harmony in the mental processes and inner conflicts are at a minimum.

One attribute within man, as we have noticed, stirs up

conflict and creates fragmentation. It is his sense of self-sovereignty, his omnipotence, his exercise of independent prerogative which he retains from his childhood. Immediate gratification of desires regardless of the voice of conscience causes a damaging split within the psyche. The immediate pleasure promises to be so satisfying that the conscience cannot restrain the will, and the person cannot say "No" or "wait."

We find that this sense of independent prerogative (a trait which only God can adequately handle) began in the Garden of Eden (Gen. 3:1-6). Satan tempted Eve to do as she pleased regardless of the law of God which forbade eating of the fruit of a particular tree (Gen. 2:17). This caused the first break in relationship with God. This was the first sin.

God had said, "In the day that thou eatest thereof thou shalt surely die" (Gen. 2:17). Death is a process of fragmentation returning to their original state elements which life has organized and built together into a whole organism. The day Adam and Eve ate the forbidden fruit they started fragmentation within God's creation, for they had separated themselves from God, the source of life, by their exercise of an independent prerogative. This is the essence of sin which causes sinful deeds—acting independently of God. (See Rom. 14:23; 1 John 3:4).

Death is always associated with sin in the Bible. "The soul that sinneth, it shall die" (Ezek. 18:4). "The wages of sin is death' '(Rom. 6:23). The subject of death in the Bible is a recurring subject. It refers to death of the soul when the soul is cut off from God, a second death (Rev. 21:8). A person is said to be spiritually dead when he is unconverted, for he is still in his sins (Eph. 2:1). Death is a process of fragmentation, a separation of unities which life has built. This understanding of death has added meaning when we think of inner security.

If one attribute derived from the nature of God functions at the expense of total unity, there is bound to be trouble, a fragmenation. Self-determination sponsors rebellion against authority. When we exercise self-determination at the expense of good judgment, we incur guilt or a serious loss of self-esteem. If we happen to feel no guilt, perhaps we will get the rejection of others who have been injurd by our conduct.

God has created all things to function in perfect harmony just as He is in harmony within Himself. Man's assertion of omnipotence, his independent prerogative, fractures this basic unity and does violence to God's design.

Man has been granted a will, for God has a will. Man has volition; God has volition. Man can choose to do as he pleases, and he does. God's design is that man should choose to do God's will and fulfill His design. If man did, he would glorify God because he would represent him faithfully. But man chooses instead to assert his own sense of sovereignty in a situation and defy his responsibility to God—he acts with self-determination. Thus the fragmentation in the universe began with Adam and Eve and has multiplied. God, being infinite in knowledge, knew it would happen and provided a means of reconciling the situation in Jesus Christ His own Son. (See 1 Pet. 1:18-21; Rev. 13:8; Matt. 25:34).

Hence, we see that man's fear of death is an innate fear. It keeps him constantly defending against life situations which might threaten his privilege of living (Heb. 2:14, 15), while at the same time he is promoting the forces of death by acting independently of God who is the source of life and wholeness.

We have an innate fear of death because there is a split within our psyche, an internal fragmentation. We can't control ourselves always to do what we know is right to do. Under strong desire and available satisfaction for that desire, we cannot always control our will to keep from indulging in the forbidden. This happens frequently in our society in matters of business honesty, sexual promiscuity, handling of the truth. It has been that way from our infancy. We all seem to know, whether we like to admit it or not, that we have a melting point, a point beyond which we cannot resist temptation. We instinctively know we can destroy ourselves by our own impulses, and many of our fears are related to this idea.

Through spiritual conversion we are restored to Him and desire His will to be done in our lives. We love Him with all our hearts—this puts Him first. The internal split is healed because the omnipotence problem is dealt with. God forgives us (Acts 10:43), makes us acceptable to His holy self (Eph. 1:6), and seals us with His Holy Spirit (Eph. 1:12, 4:30), who abides in our bodies as His temple (1 Cor. 6:19, 20). We are thus made partakers of the divine nature (2 Pet. 1:4), which cannot practice sin or fragmentation (1 John 3:9 a.s.v.). Then when our life here is over, we have the hope of being with Him eternally (John 14:1-3). At that time, all fragmentation will cease to be (1 Cor. 15:54-58).

Three critical issues

We need to focus on our priorities. Even though we may be committed to Christ and call ourselves Christian, we have within us a gravitation to the habits of the unconverted life. We continually migrate toward the sources of self-esteem which are not centered in God. We tend to return to the omnipotent position in life situations. This is hard for some Christians to understand or cope with, but the Bible does not hesitate to speak plainly about this problem, the problem of living in a constant love relationship with God where His peace reigns unwaveringly in our hearts.

Christ asks to be first in our hearts. He said to Peter, "Lovest thou me more than these?" (John 21:15). God required of the Old Testament people that they offer to Him their first fruits, the very best, their firstborn of animals, and give special sacrifices at the birth of their firstborn child. Jesus said, "Seek ye first the kingdom of God" (Matt. 6:33). Our love for God puts Him first because He first loved us (1 John 4:19), and He deserves that high position.

There are three types of pleasures which lure us away from keeping Christ first in our minds. They lure us back to our sense of independent prerogative and into a position of omnipotent thinking. They are the ways in which Satan tempts us to sin.

1. *Sensual pleasure.* If you turn again to the story of Adam and Eve (Gen. 3:6), you will notice that Satan appealed to Eve's sensual feelings to entice her to eat the for-

bidden fruit: "When the woman saw that the tree was good for food." The fruit was both appetizing and delicious.

In Matthew 4:1-11 when Jesus was tempted, Satan suggested sensual pleasure as his first attack on our Lord. "If thou be the Son of God, command that these stones be made bread." Jesus had not eaten for forty days. He was in a desert and hungry enough to eat the rocks. So Satan suggested the pleasure of eating food on his own initiative independently of God. In fact, he suggested that he demonstrate that he was the Son of God by producing the gratifying miracle. Jesus replied, "Man shall not live by bread alone, but by every word that proceedeth out of the mouth of God." Here Jesus decided to stay with the sovereignty of God and so kept God *first* by being controlled by His Word. God had given him no authority to make bread of stones, so he decided to remain hungry.

2. *Acquisition pleasure.* Again we return to Genesis 3:6. Eve noticed also that "it was pleasant to the eyes." The fruit was beautiful, a thing to be desired for its beauty, and she wanted to possess it, though actually she had no right to it.

In the second temptation of Jesus (Matt. 4:5-7), the Savior is offered something in fantasy which would be delightful to his eyes, but to which in his incarnation He had no divine authority to possess. "He shall give his angels charge concerning thee: and in their hands they shall bear thee up, lest at any time thou dash thy foot against a stone." Jesus was the Son of God and created all things. What could appeal to His desire to possess? Remember that Jesus was a lonely man. He often retired in solitude to commune with His Father. According to Hebrews 1, the angels in heaven were His preincarnate friends, ministering attentively to his needs continuously. On earth, during His incarnation, He was limited to the confines of a human body and did not take the initiative to command angels, for He was human as well as divine. Every ministration of angels to Jesus during His incarnation, you will notice, was by the initiative of His Father. He never asked for angelic help. Lonely on earth among people He knew too well to trust, Christ may have longed to view His old heavenly friends again. Conceivably it must have been tempting to jeopardize Himself by jumping from the Temple into the Kedrom Valley some 600 feet below.

But Jesus turned on Satan and said, "Thou (a fallen angel) shalt not tempt the Lord *thy* God." Jesus again put God's Word in a priority position, keeping God first ahead of the desired pleasure of visiting with and being aided by angels.

3. *Recognition pleasure.* This is a desire to be exalted. In Genesis 3:6, Eve believed that eating the fruit would make her wise. She believed that God was withholding something good from her. If she were to eat of the fruit, she would be as wise as God, knowing good and evil. She could become super-human in wisdom.

In the third temptation of Jesus (Matt. 4:8-10), Jesus is enticed to realize the ambition to be recognized or exalted. He was God, sovereign over all, but during His humiliation, that is, while on earth, He subjected Himself to the limitations of being a Nazarene, a common person. He had no social claim to anything that would make the world bow before Him and serve Him. Satan offered Him all the kingdoms of the world if He would worship him. Notice how Jesus answers this temptation: "Thou shalt worship the Lord thy God, and him only shalt thou serve." Again he quoted from the Scriptures, defending Himself against exercising a prerogative independently of God by the use of the Word of God.

These three areas of choice determine for us where our priorities actually are, whether we give God only lip service, or whether we love Him with all our hearts. *If we can stop at the point of decision and keep our priorities straight, we can maintain our intimate fellowship with God and not sin.* When an immediate sensual pleasure is available and we want it very much, but it is not right for us, we can say with Peter (John 21:15) "Yes, Lord; thou knowest that I love thee." Thus we preserve our sense of inner unity in Christ. We show our love for Christ by our obedience to Him (John 14:15). We either obey the voice of sensual pleasure or the voice of God. God does provide for sensual pleasure, but we must decide to wait until it is right according to God's word.

God gives us a right of ownership and in His providence He allows us to own certain things. These we are to receive with thanksgiving and use. We are never to love things (1 John 2:15), for when we love things, we covet. We want things for the sake of having things. Their utility value becomes mixed with our self-esteem. When the possession of delightful things or luxurious conveniences becomes a preoccupation, we are not doing the will of God.

God always resists the proud. Much is said in the Scripture about pride—the arrogance of man as he flaunts his omnipotence. God has said, "Humble yourselves therefore under the mighty hand of God, that He may exalt you in due time" (1 Pet. 5:6). When we catch ourselves being boastful, haughty, proud, we can surrender the feeling of omnipotence to God. "I love you more than the recognition of men." But when we are proud, we do not need God.

These three areas of choice are summed up in 1 John 2:15-17, where our vulnerability is contrasted with the will of God. "Love not the world . . . for all that is in the world, the lust of the flesh, and the lust of the eyes, and the pride of life, is not of the Father, but is of the world. And the world passeth away, and the lust thereof: but he that doeth the will of God abideth forever." The lust of the flesh is clearly, pleasant, physical feelings, or sensual pleasures. The lust of the eyes is the pleasure of acquisition, the desire to possess what we see that is desirable. The pride of life is the ambition to be recognized and praised by others, to be exalted.

The "will of God" is contrasted to these three critical issues. The legitimate satisfaction of these desires would be the will of God. Giving priority to a lust would put the pleasure ahead of love for God. Neither sensual pleasures, or possession of things, or recognition are worthy of man's love. Only the will of God or God Himself is worthy of man's total devotion, worthy of being *first*. Man was created in the image of God and for God, and when man is in loving relationship with God, he is complete and whole again. He is alive! He is secure.

7

Refine Your Relationships

Inner security comes from obeying the greatest of all commandments in the Bible, "Thou shalt love the Lord thy God with all thy heart, and with all thy soul, and with all thy mind" (Matt. 22:37; Deut. 6:5).

We turn our attention now to the second great commandment, which "is like unto it, Thou shalt love thy neighbour as thyself" (Matt. 22:39). We are interested in finding inner security values from obeying this second great commandment. Jesus remarked after He had given these two commandments to the inquiring lawyer, "On these two commandments hang all the law and the prophets" (Matt. 22:40). The "law and the prophets" means all the instruction for living given in the Old Testament. This summary statement of Jesus makes these two comandments actually the very center of the biblical message regarding human behavior.

There is a profound and practical truth here. In essence, Jesus was saying that the heart of living is relationship. Everything else is secondary in value to relationship with God, with others, and with self. Things provide our basic needs, and they supply a sense of security in the life situations. Food,

clothing, shelter, transportation, communication, medicine sur-
round us with some reassurance, but in spite of the fact that
things are exceedingly important to living, they cannot satisfy
the need of the human heart for a love object. "Love not . . .
things" (1 John 2:15). "The love of money is the root of
all evil" (1 Tim. 6:10).

Man can only find fulfillment in loving persons, for he is
a person who needs to be loved, and things don't love. When
we love anything less than a person, we renounce part of
ourselves and increase our insecurity. Without love our daily
defense against insecurity is to acquire enough things so we
will never want again. But the more things we acquire the
more we tend to fear we will lose them, so we need to protect
our possessions and this requires more possessions, more things
which also have to be protected. It is a never-ending vicious
cycle.

Relationships are three-dimensional

Love is the emotion of satisfying relationship. Jesus stated
clearly for us where life is. Life is relationship between persons. Life elements in man are nourished by love relationships
and these relationships are three-dimensional. All three dimensions *must* be operating for life to be satisfying. This is
the nucleus of the infinite design of God for the man He
created in His own image. God is love, and God has related
to man (Heb. 1:1, 2), and since we are in His image, we
are to relate to God and to other people and to ourselves.

Like a tripod which has no stability until all three legs
are securely planted, so man has a very shaky and unstable
relationship with other people and a flimsy inner security
until all three dimensions of his relationships are functioning.
When a person puts his trust in God and relates to Him as
his first love object, he immediately discovers a different attitude toward himself, a different source of self-esteem. This
new attitude toward himself opens the way for a more objective attitude toward others. He thinks of others as also
responsible to God whether they admit it or not. His omnipo-
ence is in God so he doesn't project it to others as he did

before. This gives him a peer feeling toward others, and peer relationships for adults are fulfilling.

The emotions which are aroused within us when we feel love toward God need to be validated in our relationships with other people. They are also in the image of God and have similar emotions. For instance, expressing love for God is a rather open-ended feeling, for God is invisible and intangible. Yet the feelings are real. We perceive other people with our five senses. They are tangible reality. When we love others and they love us, there is something empathic happening. We view their body language, we hear their voices, we feel their touch—these experiences validate to us the feelings of love which they are expressing. When we love God, who is invisible, we have none of these tangible elements in our perception of love, either to God or from God.

We read, "The love of God is shed abroad in our hearts by the Holy Ghost which is given unto us" (Rom. 5:5). In other words, when we love others in an unconditional way, we are expressing God's love, or God is expressing His love through our emotions. We may not be conscious of God doing anything at the time of our experiencing love, but, nevertheless, God is making His love tangible through us to others and through others to us. Our love for God prepares our hearts to love as God loves, unconditionally. It is the omnipotence within us that makes our love for others conditional. Therefore, relationships that are triangular in nature have a basis for security and satisfaction.

Your love for God makes your love for me unconditional. My love for God makes my love for you unconditional. Unconditional love is always acceptable and fulfilling. So in love relationships God fulfills His design for man, which is to glorify Himself, make Himself known. God's almighty power and omniscient wisdom and foreknowledge are manifested in nature, but Gods' love is manifested in man. Since man cut himself off from God in the Garden of Eden by asserting an independent prerogative to obtain what he wanted, God manifested His eternal love in human flesh through Jesus Christ, who came to redeem and restore mankind to a relationship with Himself. Our voluntary act of faith in His redemption establishes the basic relationship with God. This new relationship with God makes it possible for us to glorify Him in our love relationships with other people.

It takes all three dimensions in relationships to provide a stable inner security. If we relate to God without a loving relationship with people, we become eccentric and tend to lose contact with reality—we are religious, but not involved with life. Christ stated that He wanted His disciples to be in the world as His witnesses, His representatives. "I pray not that thou shouldest take them out of the world, but that thou shouldest keep them from the evil. . . . As thou hast sent me into the world, even so have I also sent them into the world" (John 17:15, 17). This great prayer of Christ reveals man's role in the world after he becomes spiritually converted. It is His design that we balance our relationship with God by a relationship with people. "That they also may be one in us: that the world may believe that thou hast sent me . . . that they may be one, even as we are one: I in them, and thou in me, that they may be made perfect in one" (John 17:21-23).

It is natural to receive emotional gratification from worshiping God. Worshiping God is, in a very real sense, making love to God through Christ. It is reaffirming our adoration of Him, our thanksgiving and gratitude to Him, our confession of all that we know to be wrong in our thinking and actions. It is fellowship with God in the framework of His Word and our concerns, letting our requests be known (Phil. 4:6), and rejoicing in "psalms and hymns" with others (Col. 3:16).

The euphoria of worship can accelerate into an ecstasy, and this can become a goal, an end in itself, with no particular involvement with other people. Romans 12:1-21 indicates that worship of God is intended to be a response to His unlimited mercies, but also that worship is a means of preparing our hearts to minister to other people in loving concern. First Corinthians 12:12-22 directs us in our euphoria of worship to keep our conduct orderly so that we can enhance our ministry of love to those in need. Ephesians 5:17-21 also relates worship closely with personal relationships.

It is equally a violation of God's scheme to relate to people without relating to God. We have discussed this in detail in Chapter 4 and have indicated the many hazards to our security which occur with the love-exchange principle.

The missing element in most human relationships is the personal commitment to God and the sense of fellowship with Him. This makes a very different fellowship with people possible (1 John 1:6, 7). If people have an obedient, loving walk with God in common, they have an unusual closeness to each other with the gratification of trusting and loving without qualifications.

Furthermore, God goes on to say through the beloved apostle (1 John 1:7-2:2) that the atonement of His Son continues to cleanse us from all sin. God not only establishes us by His grace in a love relationship with Himself, but He stays close at hand to maintain that relationship on a dynamic level. He continues to cleanse us from all sin the instant we admit our independent action (1 John 1:9). Since He is there functioning so dynamically to maintain the omnipotent position in each of His children, we who love Him with all our hearts are open to love each other without fear (1 John 4:18).

The apostle John refers to a "new commandment" (1 John 2:8; 3:23; 4:21; 2 John 4-6). "This commandment have we from him, That he who loveth God love his brother also (1 John 4:21). The apostle Paul referred to this commandment as the "law of Christ" (Gal. 6:2). In John 13:34, Jesus reiterates the second great commandment—the law of Christ. "A new commandment I give unto you, That ye love one another; as I have loved you, that ye also love one another." Let us investigate what it means to our emotional security to obey the "law of Christ." Such obedience will certainly refine our relationships.

A fourth level of development

In Chapter 5 we mentioned briefly that experiencing conversion started a fourth level of development. The first three levels are fundamental to the personality and they occurred very early in childhood. They were entirely involuntary.

The first level was dependency, the second, autonomy, and the third, sociability. Each level happened simply because the infant was growing and life was making more demands upon him. He was also making more demands upon the environment. In the dependency stage the child passively accepts the satisfaction of his desires. In the autonomy stage the child is actively using his initiative to satisfy his desires. He is confronted with the authority of his parents to restrict his use of intiative. This results in feelings of self-control and responsibility. In the sociability stage the child uses dependency and autonomy in the service of relating to others in social ways. He desires to be special, and in satisfying this emotional need, he must learn to limit his aggressive control of his love objects and to respect the rights and feelings of others. The drives in each of these three levels are modified by experience as the years of childhood pass until the individual is able to stand in the world as a self-confident man or woman enjoying personal relationships.

The fourth level of development is entirely voluntary. It is a spiritual level and we enter it by choice. We live it by continually reaffirming our original choice. Our decision was to love God with all our hearts, and to give Him first place— a prior claim to all that is meaningful to us. We continually reaffirm our love for Him and redetermine Him as first in our list of priorities. This is a voluntary commitment of ourselves and our lives to God, of our self-determining sense of independent prerogative to Him who has the real prerogative to do anything He chooses with our life. All of life takes on a sense of stewardship and responsibility to Him who loves us and is with us and is our source of self-esteem. We move away from claiming an essential ownership of life, that "this is *my life*," to a sense of living *His* life—He lives in and through us (Gal. 2:20).

In dependency the child related to his parents to enjoy what they voluntarily gave to him. In autonomy the child related to his environment to enjoy what he could get for himself. In sociability the child related to people to complete his feelings of identity, to enjoy being either a man or a woman. In the fourth level, spirituality, the person relates to God to discover and to enjoy his role as a vital part in God's great, eternal scheme of things. Then because he relates to God, he relates to others better because he has a better attitude toward himself. He accepts his autonomy with responsibility without having to "get his way." He exercises dependency on others more as peers than as providential parents. This fourth level gives a new motivation for being dependent, or autonomous, or sociable. The omnipotence is forwarded to God, so the person is less self-centered and more altruistic and dedicated to the welfare of others.

New orientation in social relationships

This commitment to God, which results in spiritual conversion, gives our minds a new orientation in our social relationships. Previously, we could only function socially on the love-exchange principle, as we discussed in Chapter 4.

We each need love from others to verify our feelings about ourselves. Love is a chief resource for self-esteem. If we don't receive love, we reflexively seek to support our self-esteem by defensive feelings of hostility. Hostility, in a sense, holds on to self-esteem and wards off any influence which would depreciate, then compliments itself in its success. This defensive act can be aggressively expressed, or it can assume a passive mode through self-pity, self-condemnation, and depression, as we have discussed.

We all face a variety of frustrations, rejections, and humiliations from various circumstances, and these are felt as attacks upon our omnipotence, depreciating our self-esteem largely through feelings of failure. Also, we do not always obey our conscience, or perform as we would like, in the pursuit of our desires, so from within we tend to feel guilty and self-depreciated. This internal conflict reduces our self-esteem. Therefore, we need social relationships which are supportive in nature to our sense of omnipotence to replenish our constantly deteriorating self-esteem.

The human dilemma is that every person has a similar need, some to a large degree and some to a lesser degree. Our natural solution, without God, is to exchange love. We tend to award certain people we know parental components and then maneuver to get their praise and support. In this way we unconsciously reinact situations we found satisfying in childhood or situations we wished would happen in childhood. This makes us vulnerable to criticism and rejection, and we spend much time and effort avoiding these negative reactions from others. We are not only insecure by the very nature of our self-esteem problem, but we are insecure in our resources for replenishing and maintaining our self-esteem.

Certain people, however, have entered into a love relationship with God by faith in Jesus Christ and His revealed plan of salvation from all this insecurity. They acknowledge His sovereign control of everything and submit to His Lordship. This begins a process of continually awarding Him the omnipotence. Instead of feeling omnipotent by the successful use of an independent prerogative and maneuvering others to be congratulatory, they find a self-esteem by identifying with God who is omnipotent. They love Him and submit to Him and allow Him to control them.

The love relationship with God which is supported by a total commitment to Him, satisfies the need for a pure sense of personal worth. The Christian feels right and good because he belongs to God and knows that God who owns him forgives him, making him acceptable to Himself in Jesus Christ (Eph. 1:6). Since the Christian's relationship with God is totally by His grace and not at all by any virtuous activity on his part (Eph. 2:8-10), he has a security that is based upon absolute values and is not relative to the changing factors of life situations.

This inner security positions the mind to relate to others according to an entirely new orientation. The Christian who is dependent upon God for his inner security loves others not so much to *get* love as to *give* love, and he loves others because they are persons of dignity; God loves them. His own need for self-esteem is established by his faith in God

(Rom. 12:3) and for the purpose of ministering to others (Rom. 12:4-16).

Our relationship with others after we have entered this fourth level of development, our spiritual life, is not on an exchange level. It is on an expendable level. We can love others unconditionally and expendably. We need not forwarding unreal components of authority to them to meet our own need for self-esteem. We are more able to treat them realistically as they need to be treated—as peers.

This is the will of God as stated in the second great commandment, "Love thy neighbor as thyself." Such a love is definitely a relationship between peers. The Golden Rule also states a peer relationship. "As ye would that men should do to you, do ye also to them likewise" (Luke 6:31). Several passages of Scripture indicate that we are not to be respecters of persons in our relationships. The rich are not to be exalted for their wealth; the poor are not to be exploited or dishonored because of their poverty (see James 2:1-10). The practice of a pure peer relationship outside the Christian community is almost entirely unknown, and it is more lacking among Christians that it need be.

We can have fellowship with each other as peers when we are not needing something *from* others. In Christ we are able to give *to* others because our basic need for self-esteem is met in Him. We can enjoy loving others just for the sake of having fellowship with them. Paul speaks of having a debt of love. "Owe no man any thing, but to love one another" (Rom. 13:8). We feel loved when people accept our love and relate to us lovingly. In other words, we love because we have a sense of being a person, not in order to reaffirm our feelings of worth as a person.

Jesus emphasized this truth when He asked Peter three times, "Lovest thou me more than these?" (John 21:15-17). Peter declared his love for Jesus, then Jesus added, "Feed my lambs," and "Feed my sheep." In essence Jesus said, "If you really love me, you will not be *taking* from others, but *giving* to them. Your relationship with people will be a blessing to them. If you love me, you will not be going to

people on a primary level to receive a blessing *from* them."
This condition of mind can only be possible when we have
forwarded the omnipotence to God by loving Him with all
our heart.

Inner security is available to the Christian by faith in Christ,
but this does not mean that he always feels secure. His relationship with God is established by the promises of God.
This fact does not automatically make him secure or indicate that he will always relate to others on the principle of
expendable love. He has all his social habits established from
his first three levels of maturation in the love-exchange principle where God is not a vital person in his life. His relationship *to* God is established by God as a result of the
obedience of faith in Him, he becomes His child. But his awareness of relationship *with* God may be a variable as far as his
feeling of the reality of God is concerned. The latter may be
a variable, while the former is a fixed factor. "As ye have
therefore received Christ Jesus the Lord, so walk ye in him"
(Col. 2:6). We received Christ by a voluntary act of faith;
we continue to live by a voluntary act of faith. "Be not con-
formed to this world: but be ye transformed by the renew-
ing of your mind, that ye may prove what is that good, and
acceptable, and perfect will of God" (Rom. 12:2). These
and many other verses of Scripture clearly indicate that a
Christian has to fight the undertow continually of behaving
as though he were not a Christian. When he relaxes, his old
insecurities return (see 1 Pet. 5:6-11). When he returns to
his opportunities of living in Christ, his inner security returns
and his relationship with others changes to a ministering relationship rather than one where he is seeking to be min-
istered to.

Clean up relationships by being forgiving

Since we have this established relationship with God by
faith in His promises, and He is the omnipotent One, we
are obligated to remove the stagnant pools of resentment
we hold against others.

A grudge is hostility in deep freeze. It only takes an instant under the heat of a similar situation to thaw out the old anger and to begin acting out in an accelerated way all the feelings that have been held in for years. There is a pleasure in exercising vengeance, a satisfaction which is not really satisfying. Vengeance and love are both pleasures which draw people together. Vengeance has a way of falsely reaffirming self-esteem. "I feel good. I made him pay. He suffered like I once suffered."

Since grudges and hostility are people-centered, we need to resolve these negative feelings to clean up our relationships with people. This is mandatory by the very nature of the Christian life (Eph. 4:30-32). The Christian has acknowledged God as the omnipotent One and has declared his love for God and commitment to God. Hostility, on the other hand, by its nature assumes an omnipotent position in the relationship with others. This omnipotence and its accompanying sense of independent prerogative to punish the offender is contradictory to the Chirstian's love-commitment to God.

Furthermore, it is not consistent to expect forgiveness from God for sin—sin being the assertion of an independent prerogative to act as though there were no God—when we continue to disregard God. Confessing sin and seeking forgiveness from Him acknowledges His omnipotence, His sovereignty over all in favor of our assumed right to punish, and His holiness and justice in favor of our desire to set things right ourselves.

This is why Jesus taught His disciples to pray, "Forgive us our debts, as we forgive our debtors" (Matt. 6:12), and added this explanation: "If ye forgive men their trespasses, your heavenly Father will also forgive you: but if ye forgive not men their trespasses, neither will your Father forgive your trespasses" (vs. 14, 15). It is not consistent to be forgiven of sin when we condone and practice sin and refuse to acknowledge it as sin.

God says, "Vengeance is mine; I will repay" (Rom. 12:19). This means that God is sovereign over all people, and He will discipline His own. We do not have the right to exercise vengeance over anyone. We do not have the right to feel that omnipotent.

We must understand, then, that true forgiveness of another person is not excusing him for what he has done to us, or just forgetting the whole matter. True forgiveness is committing the desire for the pleasure of vengeance to God and by faith in God's sovereign management of life situations to work out whatever is His will in the matter. When we have truly committed pleasure of our vengeance to God, we have forgiven the other person. We have forwarded our omnipotence to God and opened our minds to identify with the offending person and to love him and to communicate with him empathically. We are reconciled to him.

Though we feel reconciled to him and our love reaches toward him, we may not be able to restore fellowship with him immediately. We need his response of repentance before he is reconciled to us and good fellowship is restored. Depending upon the circumstance, we may or may not need to seek his forgiveness of us. (See Matt. 5:21-26.) It is God's will that His children be one in a spirit of loving unity.

We are His witnesses (Acts 1:8). We represent Him in our relationships with people. Luke 6:27-49 gives a brief list of all that is possible in human relationships because God is restored in the believer's heart as God. He can love his enemies (vs. 27-29). He can be generous (vs. 30-35). He can be kind and merciful (v. 35). He can be non-judgmental (vs. 37-42). He can be good and do good (vs. 43-45). He has a solid resource for inner security (vs. 46-49). We represent God when we are committed by faith to love Him. These virtues listed in this chapter of Luke are only a few of the ways we can represent God because we love Him.

Forgiving others helps to keep God first. He deserves the priority in our thinking. He must be absolutely first. We "set our affection on things above" (Col. 3:1). It is a major act of faith in God and love for God to let Him have the pleasure of our vengeance.

Reaffirm your love through generosity

Only the Christian can be truly generous, for he alone has a resource in God. God is generous because He is God; we are generous because we are "partakers of the divine nature (2 Peter 1:4).

We can be generous to be recognized and appreciated. This generosity is on the love-exchange principle. We can be generous to compensate for our guilt feelings, as though we could erase the effects of being bad by being good. We can be generous to condition fate in our favor to be kind to us in our time of future need. As an example, we may stop to be helpful to a stranded motorist and say, "Maybe someone will help me someday when I am stranded on the highway."

True generosity must be an expression of the expendable love principle, the desire to share. We are taught in the Bible to give simply because there is a need (Luke 6:32-35) and we want to minister. True love is caring when there is no thought of being repaid.

When we are truly generous because of our loving relationships with God, we have overcome the effects of greed which would cause us to hoard. We also have overcome the effects of envy which would cause us to hate anyone who has more than we have. In fact, the spirit of true generosity is a proof that we have overcome the bad effects of hostility within us. We are humble; that is, we have forwarded our omnipotence to God.

Since omnipotence is the dynamic in hostility, it is a good thing to give a generous gift to the person you have forgiven of a significant wrong as a token that you have truly forgiven him. This has a way of sealing in your own mind the transaction with God and is a reminder to you and to your reconciled friend that the offense is both forgiven and forgotten.

Delight in honoring others

The natural pride factor in each person tends to make him seek the most honored position in any social meeting. Pride is an inordinate sense of self-esteem. A proud person

is one who is self-congratulatory to the extent that he feels
better than others and regards himself as superior. He seeks
the adulation of others so he can maintain his conceit.

The proud person does not need God and he does not seek
Him. The very nature of pride is to be so reinforced in one's
own sense of omnipotence that one does not need God or
regard God with any reality. "God resisteth the proud, but
giveth grace unto the humble. Submit yourselves therefore
to God" (James 4:6, 7).

When we have submitted to God and humbled ourselves
"under the mighty hand of God" (1 Pet. 5:6), we have committed our omnipotence to Him. We reaffirm to ourselves
that we mean it when we truly delight in honoring others.

To honor others is a way of expressing love for them. "Be
kindly affectioned one to another with brotherly love; in
honour preferring one to another" (Rom. 12:10). Delight-
ing in the honor of others is another refining agent in personal
relationships to hold our fellowship away from the selfish
love-exchange principle and lock it into the unselfish expendable love principle.

But this can never happen if we honor others to satisfy
any of our own dependency needs. It is easy to respect others
as great if we need someone who is important to identify
with. "I know Mr. X. He's the most outstanding in his field."
We may need to identify ourselves with the great to feel
a bit of greatness ourselves. Or we may need someone to
assist us in our decisions or direct us in coping with our
problems, so we are quick to honor someone to gratify this
need. We wouldn't want to depend upon a person who was
not highly honored or qualified. We might even be glad to
honor another just to qualify for a compliment ourselves.
This is not the kind of honoring which forwards the omnipotence; these are all corrupted with self-centered motives.

The ideal motivation in honoring others is being truly happy
for the other person simply because he deserves the honor.
We make no comparison with ourselves, like, "I wish I were
as good," or, "I am not as good and never will be." This
ideal honoring is based upon a sense of being yourself, of

being happy that the other person is rewarded for whatever is his excellency. We might justly reason, "I have my excellencies, he has his."

Be observant, but not critical

There is a fine line between being observant of what others are doing and how they are feeling without being critical of them. But that line makes the difference between thoroughly enjoying them and only patronizing them.

Each of us has a natural defense against being labeled derogatorily. We don't mind being classified in a complimentary way, but we do not want others to think less of us than we like to think of ourselves. One of the first things we look for when we meet another person is, "What is his attitude? Is he positive or negative, respectful or critical, friend or foe?" This empathic communication of the other person's attitude immediately determines our underlying attitude toward him, whether we will be on guard or relaxed, secretive or confidential, merely intellectual in our conversation or perhaps more revealing of our true feelings.

As we have mentioned, being critical is an expression of repressed hostility. We can evaluate a person and not be critical of him. In other words, we may observe that the person is doing things of which we do not approve, or is even contradicting us; but if we love him, we will respect his self-esteem, and give him his full right. We may feel that we should say something to him about his conduct. But when we do we will be careful not to attack his self-esteem —only what he is doing. For instance, we may object to the speed a person is driving. "Did you notice how fast you are driving?" we may ask. If we are critical, we might say, "Do you want to kill us? Only a fool would drive like you do!"

The hostile person may be unconscious of being hostile, but he tends to want everyone to agree with him. If he is aware of his hostile attitude, he may welcome the fact that others differ from him, for he can then find a reason for acting out his feelings. But if he has repressed his hostility (denied that he is angry) he will want others to agree with him so he will not have to admit that he is hostile. He will expect others to view him as right and to be complimentary of his behavior and motives. He will also tend to treat others as inferior so that he can sustain his false sense of self-esteem based upon the denial of hostility.

The hostile person specializes in observing other people's faults so he can keep his own out of awareness and avoid relating to others, or being dependent upon them. He has denied his anger toward others so he only has a non-relationship feeling toward them. He may fear them, for he may unconsciously expect them to punish him for his bad attitude. His non-relationship feeling toward others naturally takes on an attitude of criticism and sarcasm just to maintain a distance for a displacement in which he is superior. At the same time he is doing this he may wonder why he is being critical and be trying to stop the non-social attitude.

A critical attitude cannot be corrected by attempts to stop being critical. When we do this, we turn on ourselves and compound the hostility with guilt feelings. It is not effective to ask God to take away the habit of being critical unless you are at the same time willing to deal with the sense of omnipotence in the spirit of criticism and give that to God. We can only stop being critical as we recognize our own hostility and non-relationship feelings. We have to see that we are acting on past grudges, many of them may be entirely unrelated to the persons toward whom we feel critical.

As we consider our attitudes, we may recognize that we are holding on to a sense of sovereignty over others that belongs only to God. We may notice that we are not really accepting His forgiveness of our sins. We are trying to justify ourselves instead of believing that His atonement is our basis of self-esteem. There is no virtue in finding fault with others. We may also correct our judgmental attitude by acknowledging that we are assuming a role with others which only God should have, that is of being the judge.

We are forbidden this privilege in clearly stated language. "Judge not, that ye be not judged. For with what judgment ye judge, ye shall be judged: and with what measure ye mete, it shall be measured to you again. And why beholdest thou the mote (tiny speck) that is in thy brother's eye, but considerest not the beam (literally, a log) that is in thine own eye?" (Matt. 7:1-3; also 4, 5).

Hostility, expressed in criticism and sarcasm, makes us relate to others without actually relating. A contact is made, but not to be helpful—all the critic is interested in is finding fault. We usually attack the person's self-esteem in ways he is totally helpless to correct. We label him as stupid, foolish, bad, ugly, ridiculous, etc. The critic shows no interest in the person's improvement; he is satisfied with being critical.

We have all been attacked by the critics who were not interested in doing anything but making us miserable. We are wary of this happening again, so we instantly, and almost unconsciously, check out another person upon contact with him to see if he is friend or foe. This emotional guard rail stands between people and seriously limits the pleasures of personal relationships.

The tendency in society to act out hostility through criticism makes actors of us all. It is most relieving to discover a person who is genuine in his love and non-judgmental in his attitudes. We find ourselves lowering our guard and opening ourselves to reveal our true feelings to that person. We naturally seek his company and enjoy sharing with him.

Being truly non-judgmental is the result of a thorough commitment of all personal omnipotence to God and honoring Him as sovereign over all people. When God is respected as Lord in life, the person is released to believe in himself. He knows he is genuine because God is genuine and has accepted him. He is identified with God in a love relationship.

Having established an inner security by his commitment to God, a Christian can accept the criticism of others objectively and not personally. He has found his basic self-esteem in the atonement of Christ, so he should not be threatened by the attacks of others upon his behavior or appearance (Rom. 8:31-39). This being established, he feels a sense of wholeness which lays the foundation for enjoying other people for the persons they are. They don't have to maintain a pleasing performance in order to qualify for love.

The two great commandments, therefore, summarize for us the basis of our own inner security and of our satisfaction in personal relationships. Because we love God with all our hearts, minds, and strength, we have found our own inner security. We are no longer dependent upon others for our self-esteem. We are able, then, to relate to them as peers, treating them as we would enjoy being treated. This opens the way for them to find in us the quality of love they would expect in God Himself—unconditional and non-judgmental. People who have such loving commitment to God, experience an expendable love for others.

In the ideal Christian fellowship there is a mutual openness with each other which brings people into a bond of unity that is indescribably fulfilling. Each trusts the other and each feels accepted by the other, regardless of what is known. Each feels accepted and forgiven by God. "If we walk in the light, as he is in the light, we have fellowship one with another" (1 John 1:7).

8

Be Self-critical But Kind

In pursuit of inner security, we need next to consider the inner world of self. We have focused our attention upon the security factors involved in relating to God and in relating to other people in a Biblical manner. Now we shall give some thought to introspection that is also Biblical in nature and its effect upon inner security.

There should be no question about the need for healthy introspection if one is to become more mature emotionally. No one matures emotionally unless he sees his errors and overcomes them in a proper way. Life is many-sided with a multitude of unexpected variables and constants, and the emphasis we make upon overcoming our errors in a proper manner is a very important consideration. Many people settle for only a partial solution to their problems.

God created all things, and God is orderly and consistent. There is a way, therefore, that considers all the variables and constants and balances the equations of life. It is reasonable to believe that there is a good way of coping with any given situation. God has revealed in the Bible that He is concerned with our problems and that He will show us that good way of coping if we exercise faith in Him. The right solution may not be what we would choose if we were to have our way independent of God, but the right solution will recognize *all* the factors involved in "I" and in "it" that need to be changed.

Insight is corrective

It is one thing to involve others in the proposed solution of a problem and quite another to discover how one is contributing to his own misery by inappropriate action. Insight is required to perceive the motivating forces in a situation, and especially to understand how one is tangling himself in his own problem.

Jim complained to me about his automobile. He said it was a lemon, that they didn't make cars like they used to. "The front end shimmies. I get poor mileage. The engine has no pep, hard to start. It's full of squeaks, and the tires wear irregularly. This is an old car with only 38,000 miles."

I asked a simple question, "How often do you lubricate it or get it tuned?"

"Oh, I never bother with that," he replied. "I don't think I've had it on the rack more than three times since I bought it new." A person does not need to know much about automobiles to understand why Jim was not happy with his car.

Mrs. Walters complained that her husband was irresponsible and failed to take the proper male leadership in the home. She did not realize that, though she thought she wanted him to be the head of the house, she was so control-oriented that he never could discover how to lead her where she wanted to go, or to ask her to do what she wanted to do.

Brad complained that his wife was unresponsive. He wondered why. He did not realize that she felt unloved and used in their marriage relationship. His responsibilities as a regional director for an auto insurance company absorbed most of his attention. He was busy encouraging his salesmen, promoting contests, and working toward having the best division in the company. He was defeating his own best interests by the way he managed his priorities.

Insight is very important to the correction of nearly every problem. Unless we understand how we are maintaining the situation we do not like, we will probably continue making the same mistakes. Insecurity is intimately related to lack of insight, for most of the problems which cause insecurity are self-perpetuating.

The hazards of introspection

Any amateur psychologist can tell a person where he is at fault when he is not involved in the problem. But it is usually very difficult for the person to see his own faults as clearly. As mentioned in an earlier chapter, we all need good self-esteem or we cannot function efficiently. Guilt is a feeling we have when we lose self-esteem. We avoid feeling guilt or blame, as much as we can, and contrive various ways of dodging guilt feelings with excuses, rationalizations, denials, etc.

Introspection is a process of investigating ourselves to find where we are at fault and to see what we can do about correcting our faults. This process is difficult for several reasons. One is our built-in tendnecy to avoid accepting blame. Another is that we need a source of self-esteem to hold to while we are being self-critical. Another difficulty is that we can easily lose all objectivity and blame ourselves excessively or distort the facts so that we do not see our own responsibility at all.

Here is a dilemma: People who have good interpersonal relationships have little insecurity and can introspect easily. People who have poor interpersonal relationships are often quite insecure and cannot introspect very well. In fact, the poorer one's relationships are with others the more he is inclined toward being defensive and insecure, and the less he can depend upon being reassured by others if he should find a fault in himself.

Every person has an abiding self-concept. We usually don't stop to think about this self-image, but it is related to a basic sense of personal worth. Personal relationships strengthen this image of self, and this supports self-esteem when we are finding fault and evaluating ourselves.

Everyone can introspect better than he thinks at first. If one thinks of himself as a sort of an "it" instead of a person among people, he will be devastated when he unveils a fault. Defective things are discarded. Defective people, however, are different. They can overcome their defects. People are not things. Besides, no one is perfect. Most everyone has defects he is working to vanquish. We can identify with our friends who have overcome, or who are presently coping with similar problems. This helps us to build a perspective on the problem we have discovered in ourselves.

We use the same avoidance techniques in our introspection that we use to avoid guilt when we are accused of something we did wrong. We rationalize. Perhaps this is the most commonly used avoidance which neutralizes an insight. We think, "I may be wrong, but I'm not the only one." By sharing guilt, we do not seem to feel as guilty. "I'm a product of my environment—look at the childhood I had." This diverts attention from the responsibility for changing to some past situation or to someone else.

Another rationalization is to ask "Why?" "I wonder why I'm like this?" Again this diverts our attention to some explanation for the condition instead of how it can be met and overcome. After a little progress is made in overcoming the problem, the reason why may be much more meaningful.

We offer excuses. This neutralizes the value of corrective insight. "I can't help it" is one very common excuse. We often hear people openly declare their personality problem and then conclude with, "That's the way I am." They have insight but do nothing about changing because they draw the picture of themselves with, "That's the way I am," which implies, "That's the way I want to stay." Perhaps they will say, "I have a bad temper. It doesn't take very much to set me off, but I don't hold grudges. After I've said it, I forget it." He gives no thought to what he is doing to others and his need to cope with frustration differently.

We exaggerate. We are aggravated because something is

wrong with us, and we do not feel sensible showing our anger, so we express the irritation by exaggerating the fault. It is as if we could punish someone by making ourselves bad. When this attitude prevails in introspection, we lose sight of the real problem and become lost in our sense of badness. The theme is: "If I'm not perfect, then I'm nothing —I refuse to acknowledge any goodness in myself, for there will probably be a defect in it also. I can never be good, so why try?"

Sonja had been a widow for six years and she missed her husband very much, especially around the anniversaries of his death. Her loneliness and grief made her introspective in a bad sense of the word. She not only recalled nostalgically many pleasant experiences with her husband, but she also thought about how she might have been a better wife. She became depressed over her memories as though she had completely failed her husband. Her recall in this regard was not of certain situations, but more of a picking at little things in which she assumed she had failed him.

The anger in her mood was related to loneliness and to feeling forced to accept widowhood. She was also angry at the way her married friends seemed to make her feel unwelcome in their company now that she had no husband. She had no object at which to strike in the situation, so her anger made her feel depressed. She expressed her anger by grossly distorting the facts and insisting to herself that she was a failure. She wanted to give up and just quit living.

There are other people who are not as overt as Sonja in feeling depressed and discouraged with living. They avoid introspection because they fear they might get into a bad mood like Sonja. Their attitude is, "I'm afraid to look inside myself. I may find so much wrong I will never be able to correct it all. I could never live with myself if I ever discovered how miserable I really am."

Looking inside can be a serious threat to self-esteem, but the person who says this is making the mistake of expecting to overcome everything all at once. We can only correct what we know to be wrong, and in God's mercy, He only shows us a little at a time. Our minds are so constructed that we will never be aware of more fault in ourselves than we can actually cope with emotionally. It may seem like it is too much, but we have natural defenses against an overload, and our minds block against comprehending beyond a certain point.

The time factor in introspection is important. Is the deficiency something related to childhood and now part of the life style? Of is it something that has recently developed? If it is a life style problem it will be more difficult to overcome and will take a little longer.

We also must remember that when we sense a fault in ourselves we begin to feel anxious. We tend to become impatient. We want the problem corrected immediately. It takes time and self-discipline to overcome most emotional conflicts, and the fact that the fault has been acknowledged is an important step in correcting it. Most of our emotional problems only exist because we have no cognizance of what they really are. As soon as we capture an insight, we usually begin to institute changes. The tendency is to see a little change and then relax before the whole problem is overcome.

Introspction and faith

We have the ability to stand off and look at ourselves as though we were able to step outside our bodies and be our own critic. In this introspection, the question of sovereign authority becomes immediately important. If we do not happen to be spiritually converted, we will naturally assume that we are alone in our introspection, that we belong solely to ourselves. This sense of self-ownership conditions how we handle our insights. If, on the other hand, we are spiritually converted, we will take a different view of ourselves when we introspect. We will not feel alone in judging ourselves, but we will sense God's presence, talking to us about our condition. We will feel responsible to Him, but since He loves us and has forgiven us, our relationship with Him will give us courage to follow through on our insights. We have the basic self-esteem we need in order to view ourselves more objectively and see our faults.

The Christian has made God his sole owner. He has been judged and pronounced guilty by God, and he has accepted this verdict. The believer has accepted God's provision of pardon through the death and resurrection of Christ for sin. He is committed to God as one who has been raised from the dead "to walk in newness of life" (Rom. 6:4). His self-esteem is established by his faith-walk with God as he obeys the Word of God. He is assured that "there is therefore now no condemnation to them which are in Christ Jesus" (Rom. 8:1). From this self-concept he can view his faults with an objective attitude and find God's grace to help overcome them.

Introspection for a Christian is standing off and looking at himself critically, but not alone. There is One who stands with him to reassure him and give him hope that he can do the right thing. He can criticize himself and be functioning in his own best interests, but he is not seeking insight in order to be a better person just so he can glory in his improvement. He seeks rather to glorify God. Thus a Christian can introspect profitably, for he has a vital relationship with God supported by the changeless Word of God to hold on to while seeking new insights into his own faults.

In 1 Corinthians 13, Paul discusses the importance of love in the Christian life. He concludes by stating, "Now abideth faith, hope, and love, these three; but the greatest of these is love." The Christian is a person who lives by faith in God. This faith opens the way for a vital relationship with God which gives him hope in facing the vicissitudes of life, courage to overcome his deficiencies because he has the hope of mastering them, and the anticipation of being rewarded for his faithfulness when he begins his life with God in the new heaven and the new earth. All of this is made possible through love—God's love for us, and our love response to His love.

Attitudes which inspire insight

Life is growth. There is no stopping place, no zenith of achievement in the scale of possible perfection. God has made us in such a way that to stop growing is to stop enjoying being alive. If we consider ourselves mature enough to handle any situation, it will not be long before some new problem will occur which will overwhelm us. We have to grow to keep up with life. When we stop growing, we become consumed with insecurities.

Insight is at work when we admit that we are a growing person. As long as we live we expect to be growing to higher plateaus of emotional maturation. This attitude helps to cancel the deadly effects of unrealistic idealization. Instead of being discouraged by some deficiency because the ideal fantasy of our own perfection was smashed, discovering a deficiency has a sense of challenge. If we never expect to get "there," we will not be so devastated when we discover that we are not "there" yet, but there is a sense of accomplishment in the journey.

A second guiding attitude which inspires insight is to acknowledge your problem and not blame something else. Own it as your responsibility to correct. Think how you can attack it to overcome it. Keep your mind on the correction, not on rationalization, excuses, or exaggeration.

A third guiding attitude which inspires insight is to avoid making comparisons with others. We are personally responsible to God for ourselves. When Peter attempted to compare himself with John, Jesus responded emphatically, "If I will that he tarry till I come (referring to his second coming), what is that to thee?" (John 21:23). If we take the attitude that Paul recommended in Romans 14, "Whether we live, we live unto the Lord; and whether we die, we die unto the Lord: whether we live therefore, or die, we are the Lord's" (v. 8), we will be more open to the insights that God will reveal.

A fourth guiding attitude which inspires insight is a commitment to God in daily living. A personal relationship with God establishes a sense of worth because of His forgiveness and acceptance. His ownership gives Him the right to guide our minds in self-criticism, for His goals are always good. It is the ministry of the Holy Spirit in us to convict us of sin, and to make us into the image of Christ. We can accept our deficiencies more readily if we sense a loving Heavenly Father pointing them out to us for our good and His glory.

Overcoming bad memories

We have all had experiences we would like to forget. Some people seem to forget better than others, but actually the mind never forgets an experience. We may lose the power of immediate recall, but when a proper association is made, the memory returns—usually as a brief thought at first, then later with more complete details.

Since little is ever forgotten, it is logical to assume that our present behavior is constantly being influenced by past memories. We decide to go to the beach, for instance. Immediately we picture ourselves already there, so we dress for the occasion, take our sun glasses and perhaps a camera or a ball or an umbrella. The idea of a beach visit brought many other ideas from our library of memories, and we prepared accordingly. Even the idea of going to the beach itself may have been a problem-solving deduction based upon past experiences recorded in the memory bank. The day was hot, perhaps, and we thought of cooling off at the beach where we had previously found relief.

Our eating habits are a result of memory. A thousand and one childhood experiences have been recorded, and so our reflex actions have been trained to eat according to certain rules of etiquette. Habits of dressing, modesty, bathing, toileting, etc., are all evidence of the influence of past memories on present conduct.

There are good memories, and there are bad ones. Traumatic experiences are remembered more easily and have a greater influence upon us than pleasant ones. We are pleasure oriented, so anything that has been painful will be feared or avoided. We recoil from hot surfaces, cold objects, wet paint, and high voltage. We automatically associate bad-tasting substances with medicine.

This is why the process of repression takes place. There has been a traumatic experience in the past which associates unconsciously with what is presently occurring. Many of these repressed ideas are associated in the mind with memories of parental authority and become a part of what is known as the superego, or conscience. This controlling function of the mind influences us to want what is good and to reject what is bad. Briefly, it helps us conform to social custom and to the law of God.

The life of June, a teen-ager, shows how forgotten memories control present conduct. June wanted to go to the movies to see a certain show that her friends had been raving about. Just as she was getting ready to leave for the theater, company arrived unexpectedly, and it was obvious that she could not go to the show. She was both frustrated and angry, but she could not express her feelings with the company present. Traumatic memories she had forgotten in childhood of punishment and humiliation for expressing herself freely in front of guests caused her to repress her anger. It was as though she would be punished again if she showed her guests how she really felt. Instead, she instantly told them how glad she was to see them and did her best to make them welcome. When she stopped to think of it, she could tell she was denying an opposite emotion, for she felt so compelled to make them welcome she wondered if she might not be overdoing it.

June did not recall any of the childhood memories specifically which influenced her reaction, but she behaved as though she had remembered. As soon as her guests departed, June felt in an ugly mood, ready to strike out at any little frustration. We don't always understand immediately why we behave as we do, because the details of the controlling traumatic memory are repressed beyond immediate awareness.

Most of us got a little mixed up when we were on the assembly line of childhood. Some elements were omitted that should have been installed, and some were implanted that never should have been included. Childhood has pro-

vided many good memories, useful experiences, helpful ex-
amples. But also we all have empty spaces in our personalities,
hungers that have never been realized, defensive attitudes
that need to be removed, attitudes that are unrealistic. We
have habits of reacting that we wish we could change. Many
of us have adopted values, priorities, and goals that are
false. Often we are unaware of our own capabilities because
we are so busy with the unimportant and non-essential.

Most of us need new experiences to displace the old, new
impressions to take the place of false impressions of childhood. Most everyone could use a few new attitudes and
would appreciate a little insight to find a new perspective.

Everyone's story validates in some way the lasting influences of parents upon their children for good or evil. The
Bible says, "Train up a child in the way he should go:
and when he is old, he will not depart from it" (Prov. 22:6).
The good influences of the parents upon the impressionable
mind of the growing child are lasting, and so are the bad.

A parent's uncontrolled anger can have damaging effects
on children's emotional maturation. This is probably one of
the most common offenders. Harvey, for instance, was often
intimidated and terrified by his father's violent temper. At
forty-three Harvey had done practically nothing useful with
his life. He had difficulty controlling his impulses. He seldom
made good decisions, and it was hard for him to remember
his promises. The father's anger tantrums may not have been
the only contributing factor, but they led the way.

A bossy, demanding mother can be a leading cause of
procrastination in the adult. This trait can also develop sons
into being passive, compliant males who are not equipped
as adults to be the head of their homes. They continually
relate to their wives as they once did to their mothers.

Another childhood experience which disturbs the security
of adulthood is unresolved guilt over childhood sexual curi-
osity, which in itself had no moral value. A great degree of
insecurity develops when a child has been molested by an
adult or observed too much sexual exposure too soon.

Nancy was sexually molested by her grandfather several

times between the ages of nine and eleven. At the time it happened, she could not tell her parents, for she feared their wrath. She liked her grandfather and she somewhat enjoyed what he did, but she felt guilty and very ashamed. Nancy, at twenty-seven, only dated men she considered disqualified for marriage. She was afraid of desirable men. She also was inclined to favor men much older than herself. Nancy needed to overcome some bad memories, and I am happy to report that she did.

Sometimes children are unwanted. The unwanted child is a problem to the parent from the moment of conception. The parent may try to conceal the rejection, may even repress the idea that the child is unwanted, but the message is communicated to the child long before he reaches adulthood.

Alma, for instance, was overprotective of her six-year-old son. He deeply resented her smothering attention. He wanted to stand alone and do things for himself, take the chances other boys took, and be a man. Alma thought she loved him almost inordinately, for he was on her mind continuously, her only child. Her son knew he was rejected, for she interfered with his activities in a way that implied that he was still a baby. In counseling, Alma discovered that she was overprotecting him to keep him from supposed danger because she was afraid something would happen to him that would fulfill her secret wish for him to be gone. It took a while before Alma could get in touch with her real feelings about her son. When she did, she immediately showed a loving attitude toward him that respected his individuality. She also discovered that the reason she did not want him in the first place was due to some bad memories she had in her childhood. Her parents had unwittingly given her the message that it was a disgrace to be pregnant, and she felt ashamed of the evidence that she and her husband had sexual activity.

The memory of a dear woman comes to mind. Carol was born into a large family. She was unwanted from birth. Her parents arranged for a neighbor lady to take care of her when she was very small. The neighbor could have no children of her own, and she became attached to Carol. She moved across town taking Carol with her as her own. Carol's parents did not pursue to recover their daughter, and Carol rarely saw her parents after that.

As she grew up, Carol's foster mother refused her any playmates; she must always be near her foster mother where she could be seen and be of service. Carol must always hurry home from school and be attentive to her chores. She was constantly told that her parents did not want her and that she owed her life to her foster mother. The girl felt both despised and possessed by her foster mother. Carol recalled no experience of feeling loved by anyone, but she could see others relating at a distance in loving ways and wondered curiously what it was like. During her teen-age years she was told that she was not to expect to do anything in life but to take care of her foster mother in her old age.

Carol felt inescapably trapped, and she deeply resented it. At eighteen, however, her foster mother was stricken with cancer and died. This left Carol, an adult, all alone, without being prepared to relate to other people or to find a life of her own. Her wish for freedom seemed to be fulfilled, but she didn't know what to do with it.

But Carol didn't let her problem overwhelm her. She cautiously tried to relate to some people she knew better than others and found them friendly. She was always told that she should not talk to people, for no one would like her, and she would only be a bother to them. But Carol began to prove that these ideas were all wrong. She wondered what a church was like, and fortunately she began attending one that did not hesitate to preach the Gospel of saving grace and the love of God. Carol was spiritually converted and discovered a community of people in the church who accepted her, but it was difficult for her to believe they wanted her or meant their love. Carol's faith in God did not suddenly erase all the effects of her bad memories, but her faith did give her a new sense of identity and a courage to face her problems.

In adulthood, we all awaken to the fact that either we

are insecure with a shaky sense of identity, or we have a fairly substantial peace of mind and are able to get by. It is good to know, however, that a person's sense of being a whole person is not a fixed factor he must always live with. On the contrary, it is usually quite variable and can be changed considerably by taking certain remedial steps.

One fact is important. If we have some bad memories as adults, we can only overcome them if we take the responsibility for them. It does no good to blame the person who offended us. We may need to talk about the offender to get at our repressed anger, but we cannot discharge the anger if we continue to project the blame.

The problem may have begun during impressionable years, before we could rationalize and reason, but now we are not so impressionable, and we can rationalize and reason, and we are responsible for ourselves. So casting blame on parents or on anyone else only perpetuates the problem. If one is suddenly in water over his head, it does no good to raise his fists in anger and blame the person on the bank who pushed him in. He had better start swimming to get out.

Another important factor is distortion. Childhood memories are often distorted with misconceptions of the situation, the effects of deep feelings of vengeance or fear, and the impressions one has accumulated by retelling the incident. Nearly every story tends to drift from the true facts every time it is retold, embellished with imaginary elements.

In resolving bad memories and trying to get in touch with forgotten feelings, it is often helpful to confide in a trusted friend. If the friend will be slow to speak and quick to listen and not give analytical interpretation and advice, relating old experiences can be a most therapeutic thing to do. The problem with telling another person is that usually he will say, "That's ridiculous! I don't see why you are so upset about that." Or he'll take the opposite view, "Oh, I don't know how you stood it. It makes me angry just to hear you tell about it. He *ought* to suffer for that." If the friend will just listen, you can get in touch with feelings you probably would never recall if you were to think about the experience alone.

Having availed yourself of a new awareness of all that happened in the past traumatic experience, you can now feel differently about it all. With a new perspective on your feelings, you are now an adult. You were a child when it happened. Talking about it brought the childhood feelings into more mature points of reference. You can also forgive anyone who has hurt you and against whom you have been holding a grudge. Perhaps you were not aware of the bad feelings against a certain person until you took the trouble to recall all that happened.

Think positively and realistically

Most of us are aware of two patterns of thinking in our society. One is positive, the other negative. The positive pattern is optimistic and constructive. The negative is pessimistic and destructive.

The positive person tends to overemphasize the good, the hopeful, and the pleasant. He devaluates opposing ideas. The negative person tends strongly to emphasize only things that are wrong, to point to the impossible, and to discourage efforts in trying to improve. Negative thinking magnifies the cost of success and complains about the problems and the impossibilities involved in trying.

Life is full of problems. It is not all good nor is it all bad. It is a combination of good and evil, success and failure, hope and impossibilities. The positive person tends to emphasize the desirable and reject the undesirable. The negative person has trouble believing that anything will be desirable. Both need to practice thinking realistically.

It is consistent with Christian faith to think more positively even though the believer is combating many problems, for he is vitally related to God, who cannot fail. God is in sovereign control and He is leading. It is inconsistent for a professing Christian to practice negative thinking, for the Bible contradicts the basis for this pattern in many passages.

Positive thinking requires effort and attention; negative thinking happens easily without trying. Negative thinking is based upon resentment against any situation that is not pleasing. Such resentment is usually a pattern of reacting since childhood. There is no gratitude, for nothing is quite as expected. The resentment is usually expressed and manifests itself in a complaining, pessimistic attitude about almost everything.

It is annoying to be around a negatively oriented person. The only consolation might be that if you are also negative you can share your complaints and fellowship this way. But if you are inclined to think positively, it is difficult to relate to a chronically negative person.

The person who habitually thinks negatively does not expect good to happen. When it does, he is apprehensive about how long it will last. He is so preoccupied with the possibility of another disappointment that he overlooks the value of getting what he really wants.

To think positively, on the other hand, has true value for one can more fully enjoy the good while it exists; he is not so concerned about losing it that he is unable to appreciate it gratefully.

The ability to formulate good decisions requires consistent habits of positive thinking. Negative thinking sets no goals but seems to attack the goals that others set. Positive thinking sets goals and dreams of what might happen. The negative person is too preoccupied with the impossibilities involved to do that.

People normally possess a quality of reliable judgment by which they can review what they have learned from past experiences and project that knowledge toward the imagined future to develop a procedure which might succeed. A positive attitude of mind makes it possible to think more clearly and objectively, and as a result, to make better decisions. On the other hand, a negative, doubtful, pessimistic attitude will automatically and quite unconsciously, build certain elements into any decision which predestinate a disappointment or possibly a failure.

A negatively oriented person does not expect to make good decisions. Often he gets what he expected, and this has a way of undermining his courage to correct his errors, and it has a way of perpetuating his tendency to be negative. While he thinks he is protecting himself from possible hazards by noting the difficulties, he is actually promoting his own insecurity. He remains in his negative attitude and misses many fulfilling experiences.

The person who habitually thinks positively is quite aware of both his strengths and his weaknesses. He believes he can win by doing his best. This expectant attitude draws allies on the basis of his confident radiance. Each time he succeeds in a situation he verifies his own positive attitude and increases his measure of self-esteem. This gives him more reason to continue thinking positively. If he should experience a failure, he will tend to be more cautious in his consideration of the facts before he makes other decisions in the future. So we see that positive thinking prepares the mind to learn from life's disappointments.

The person with a negative mental attitude is unwilling to risk the adventure of being positive. It is natural for anyone to fluctuate at times from positive to negative in his mental attitudes, but the person who seldom thinks positively seems to resent the fact that life expects him to take chances. He fosters a dependency upon others and tends to harbor a vexation if they do not cooperate to provide him the safety he desires. He places too much responsibility upon "it" and assumes too little responsibility for "I." The dynamic balance between "I" and "it" is disturbed.

The negatively oriented person has not only disturbed the balance between "I" and "it" but has caused a split within himself which destroys his own sense of wholeness. His fear of failure and of possible inferiority cause him to rely excessively upon "it" for success. This dependency is a denial of his latent need to feel independent initiative. He cannot find much self-esteem from accomplishments that others have made possible for him when he knows he should have done these things by himself.

Until the person receives insight into what he is doing to himself when he gives in to his fear of being responsible for his own decisions, he will tend to compensate for the unwholesome feelings by various depreciating ideas, such as, "I never do anything right," "I'm no good," "I can't win." When he expresses ideas about himself that are negative, he is blindly bidding for the sympathetic indulgence of others.

If he succeeds in such manipulation, he may be momentarily gratified but not satisfied, for within himself there is a dim awareness that he is not resolving his problem. But because he did succeed in getting someone to make life a little easier, perhaps to remove some of the risk involved in a courageous decision, he must remain unhappy and dependent in order to do it again. Apparently, the price of appearing inadequate and somewhat dependent does not seem as great as the price of being courageously responsible for himself and for his decisions.

The heart of the problem lies in the basic resentment the negative person feels about anything in life that is not pleasing. He shows this resentment by complaining and being pessimistic. He also expresses his hostility by resenting others who are not sympathetic with him, and he spites them by refusing to try to help himself any more than he already does. The resentment closes his mind to learning from life's problems a better way of coping. He continually promotes his own insecurity.

A third pattern of thinking that promotes insecurity must be considered seriously here. It is neither positive nor negative in nature, but it is self-deceptive.

Because the person has not matured properly in his childhood, he has a bad self-image. He honestly believes that he is inferior, that he is nothing, or close to it. Such a self-concept is impossible to live with, for it gives a person no premise from which to function. He may have developed this idea about himself from parents who were overly critical, but that is not always the case. Each person who practices this pattern of self-deception seems to have his own set of reasons for the conclusion that he is nothing.

Since he honestly believes that his personal worth is nearly zero, he sets about to deny this fact and to prove to himself that it is not so. He is usually a perfectionist in what he does and how he appears. He must capture the concern and admiration of others to feel value in himself. There must be no flaw, for any criticism that others may make of him only verifies to him his basic self-image, that he is nothing and inferior to everyone.

Notice that the structure is self-deceptive. He does not admit that he has certain deficiencies and that he is trying to overcome them so that he will be better. He is trying to prove to himself that he has no deficiencies, for to him any observable deficiency disqualifies him for the admiration of others and verifies his basic belief about himself.

The solution to this pattern of self-deception is to be realistic about oneself and acknowledge that there are both strengths and weaknesses—that he is neither but both. He can improve if he will stop being angry, quit comparing himself with others, and try to improve whatever deficiency he knows about for the sake of becoming better, not to prove that he is something, or not "nothing."

Size up your "shoulds"

A practice which causes internal conflict and much insecurity is trying to obey a list of "shoulds" we have set up for ourselves. "I should read my Bible." "I should pray more." "I should be on time." "I should feel love for my wife." "I should feel responsive to my husband." "I should be submissive to my husband." "I should be kind to others." The list is endless.

Each of these "shoulds" is a worthy ambition. We even design the list ourselves, but after we make the list, we find that we are forcing ourselves to do something we genuinely do not feel like doing. Then, we usually browbeat ourselves with guilt feelings trying to motivate action. Sometimes we do and often we don't obey our "shoulds." We just aren't "with it."

The ambition, "I should write a letter to mother," sounds good the first or second time one says it to himself. But after that the "I should write a letter to mother" becomes an accusation of neglect. The answer to the dilemma is, "What do you *want* to do?" We may reply, "I should write a letter, but I really don't want to right now." "Then if that's the case, don't write until you want to." But the reply is, "But I *should* write. She expects a letter."

Now we are on the way to some insight. We should write because mother expects it, but we don't want to just now because we want to write when *we* feel like it. We are still trying to be independent of mother to do what we want without her prompting us. "But mother isn't here," we reason. "Yes she is—in our minds. We can't be ourselves until we liberate ourselves from this parental "should" feeling.

"And how can I do that?"

The answer is simple, much easier to explain than it is to do consistently. First ask yourself, "What is right? Do I want to do what is right? Is it right to be right?" You may answer, "It is right for me to write mother. I want to do what is right, and it is right to be right. It is *my* right that I want to do, not *mother's*." In this way you can get a feeling about what you *should* do that makes it what you *want* to do. If you truly want to be right, then you will do right for your own gratification in knowing that right has been done.

In the meantime, ask yourself if your letter to mother is because you really love her or because you want to please her. There is a vast difference. This may help you to feel that the letter represents you and your love, not just what may please mother because mother expects to hear from you.

Reading your Bible, praying, feeling love for wife, being submissive and responsive to husband—all these and others can be handled the same way. The deed is not the prime issue. The feeling of acting independently of parents is the prime issue. The deed is important, so we blame ourselves because the deed is not done. We overlook the fact that the negligence satisfies the need to feel independent of the parent through the "should." By uncovering our true feelings, we can claim the issue as belonging to us and we can handle it much better.

Stabilize your faith in God

Two great commandments are presented in the Bible as being fundamental to all meaningful relationships (Matt. 22: 37-40). From these commandments we gather that loving God with all our heart, soul, and mind is the most fundamental relationship we can ever have. It orients us to infinite reality in a primary way.

If we obey the first great commandment, we give to God the omnipotence which continually led us into sinning against Him and our neighbors and so undercut our inner security. This relationship with God is possible through the redemption that is graciously provided by God through Jesus Christ as a manifestation of His love for us. When we reach out to God in response to His love for us, we become spiritually converted, and this establishes for us an entirely new sense of inner security. Our security is based upon the changeless Word of God, the Bible, and God Himself, who is infinite, absolute, and changeless.

Being Christians in the true biblical sense of the term, we have a new premise for self-esteem through identification with God, who is omnipotent and sovereign. We are no longer dependent upon others for our primary resource of self-esteem. This delivers us from the futile bondage of the love-exchange principle in human relationships and liberates us to function more on the expendable love principle to care for others as God cares, unconditionally.

Also, being Christians gives us a new attitude toward ourselves so that we can overcome our own inner conflicts much better. We have a new promise for self-esteem which gives us a grip on identity while we examine ourselves critically to discover our faults and deficiencies. We also have God's leadership through His Holy Spirit and His Word in overcoming the faults and deficiencies we uncover. This makes it possible to overcome our immaturities and develop better ways of thinking and coping with life's problems. We can introspect safely, realistically, and constructively because of our faith in God.

But faith in God needs strengthening and stabilizing. Jesus

often commented about the little faith of his disciples. He acknowledged the great faith of the centurion (Luke 7:9). Jesus promised that great things could happen if we had faith as a grain of mustard seed (Matt. 17:20). Faith in God is primary. Faith relates us to God, the Author of life. It is only by faith that we can please God (Heb. 11:6).

Faith in God puts the omnipotence where it belongs—in God; hope in God (Ps. 42:5) puts the omnipotence where it belongs—in God; and love for God puts the omnipotence where it belongs—in God. "Now abideth these three: faith, hope, and love" (1 Cor. 13:13). These three are the basic attitudes of the Christian in his relationship with God.

With these three attitudes, we are ready to relate to others in Christian love as 1 Corinthians 13 indicates that we should. But notice that this Godly love has an altruistic quality of being expendable. It is not the least self-centered in its nature. This can happen if we love God as the first great commandment admonishes.

Faith in God must be cleansed of the "give me" spirit and be filled with the "use me" spirit. We do have requests to make of God, and we receive much from God for which we are thankful, but the motive of asking from God needs also to be used in His service to represent Him to others.

As indicated in Chapter 7, our relationship with God is not only for self, it is also to represent Him, to serve Him, to witness of His grace and power. Jesus said the way to be a great disciple (that is to be spiritually mature) is to serve others and to minister to their needs. (See Mark 10:43, 44; Luke 10:36, 37; John 13:14; 21:16; Gal. 6:2, 10).

This truth is demonstrable. As we study the Bible seeking a personal message from God and to be taught of Him about the vicissitudes of life, our faith grows (Rom. 10:17). As we encounter others who are in distress and seek to represent God to them, our faith grows. As we seek God's leadership in both our daily duty and in our Christian service, our own faith grows. Every person who has some specific ministry for Christ discovers his faith growing as he seeks to meet the needs that come to his attention.

James gives us a fitting conclusion to our thinking on this subject. "My brethren, count it all joy when ye fall into divers temptations; knowing this, that the trying of your faith worketh patience" (James 1:2, 3). Patience is the ability to accept what you don't like without becoming resentful.

Then he adds, "But let patience have her perfect work, that ye may be perfect and entire, wanting nothing" (v. 4). "For when your patience is finally in full bloom, then you will be ready for anything, strong in character, full and complete" (*The Living Bible*). When this happens, a person has found inner security!

Subject Index

Scripture Index